This Dialogue of One

First published in 2014 (hardback)
Second printing 2015 (paperback)
by Eyewear Publishing Ltd
Suite 38, 19-21 Crawford Street
London, W1H 1PJ
United Kingdom

Graphic design by Edwin Smet
Author photograph by Kate Bomford
Printed in England by TJ International Ltd, Padstow, Cornwall

Set in Bembo 12 / 14,5 pt
ISBN 978-1-908-998-880

WWW.EYEWEARPUBLISHING.COM

This Dialogue of One

MARK FORD

Essays on Poets from John Donne to Joan Murray

👓 **EYEWEAR** LITERARY CRITICISM

By the same author

poetry
Landlocked (1992)
Soft Sift (2001)
Six Children (2011)
Selected Poems (2014)

biography and criticism
Raymond Roussel and the Republic of Dreams (2000)
A Driftwood Altar: Essays and Reviews (2005)
Mr and Mrs Stevens and Other Essays (2011)

translation
New Impressions of Africa by Raymond Roussel (2011)

Contents

Preface

My title for this collection of essays comes from John Donne's 'The Extasie'. The poem presents two lovers seated on a bank engaging in a complex but wordless communication; their hands are 'firmely cimented / With a fast balme' and their 'eye-beames' are so twisted together that it is as if their eyes are threaded 'upon one double string'. In this immobile state, their bodies paralyzed 'like sepulchrall statues', their souls set about negotiating with each other. The poem offers a series of ingenious figurations that attempt to define the spiritual nature of their passion, but Donne characteristically concludes that it would be wrong for the lovers to neglect their bodies entirely. Even 'pure lovers soules', he explains, must descend

> T'affections, and to faculties,
> Which sense may reach and apprehend,
> Else a great Prince in prison lies.

This turn to the physical is not only desirable in itself, but is likely to enable less sophisticated lovers ('Weake men') to understand and learn from their love. Donne also, though, imagines in the poem's final quatrain a lover who is as refined as the entranced pair; he has somehow overheard their unspoken conversation, and agrees with the speaker's argument that the use of their bodies will dilute little, if at all, the spiritual purity of their rapture:

And if some lover, such as wee,
  Have heard this dialogue of one,
Let him still marke us, he shall see
  Small change, when we'are to bodies gone.

Reading, it seems to me, can also often feel like a dialogue of one. The writer is not there, but all the reader's experiences and expectations and tastes and sense of identity are in dialogue with the author's written words in a manner that is analogous to the silent communication that 'The Extasie' depicts. And, in turn, the process of writing about what one has read can seem rather like the turn to the body in the second half of Donne's poem. 'Loves mysteries in soules doe grow', Donne's speaker insists, 'But yet the body is his booke'.

Readerly passion can find written expression in all manner of ways, from the diary entry ('One of the best books I have ever read', I infallibly observed in a journal I kept in 1974 of every Nevil Shute or Desmond Bagley novel that came my way) to the most elaborate academic exegesis. Most of the pieces collected here were first published in the *London Review of Books* and the *New York Review of Books*, and I am grateful to my editors there, Daniel Soar and Bob Silvers respectively, for commissioning them. The exceptions are the essays on James Thomson (the alcoholic Victorian poet rather than the 18th-century author of *The Seasons*), which was commissioned by Matt Bevis for the *Oxford Handbook of Victorian Poetry*; the essay on Samuel Greenberg and Hart Crane, which was written for *New Walk*; and the one on Joan Murray, which was first published in *Poetry*.

Fevers of the Bone: John Donne

John Donne preached his final sermon as Dean of St Paul's on 25 February, 1631, the first Friday of Lent. 'And when', his early biographer Izaak Walton records in his *Life*, 'to the amazement of some beholders he appeared in the Pulpit, many of them thought he presented himself not to preach mortification by a living voice but mortality by a decayed body and a dying face. And doubtless many did secretly ask that question in *Ezekiel; Do these bones live?*' Donne's text was taken from Psalms, 'And unto God the Lord belong the issues of death', and the sermon, published the following year as *Deaths Duell*, delivered a sustained and harrowing meditation on mortality. Our time in the womb, and birth itself, are vividly interpreted in terms of death:

> Wee have a winding sheete in our Mothers wombe, which growes with us from our conception, and wee come into the world, wound up in that *winding sheet*, for we come to *seeke a grave*.

Nor does Donne flinch from describing the physical decay of a corpse, its *'putrefaction* and *vermiculation'* (i.e. its being eaten by worms). Even 'the *children of royall parents*, and the *parents of royall children'*, he reminds King Charles I, who was in the congregation in the chapel at Whitehall that day, must suffer the indignities of having their flesh promiscuously, indeed incestuously, intermingled with that of other corpses, until all traces of individual identity are dissolved:

> *Miserable riddle*, when the *same worme* must bee *my mother*, and
> *my sister*, and *my selfe*. *Miserable incest*, when I must bee *maried* to
> my *mother* and my *sister*, and bee both *father* and *mother* to my
> *owne mother* and *sister*, *beget*, and *beare* that worm which is all that
> *miserable penury*; when my *mouth* shall be *filled* with *dust*, and the
> *worme* shall *feed*, and *feed sweetely* upon me…

According to Walton, 'many that then saw his tears, and heard
his faint and hollow voice' expounding these elaborately
gruesome arguments decided that 'Dr. Donne *had preach't his
own Funeral Sermon*'.

In a letter of the previous month to his friend George
Garrard, Donne had confessed it was his 'desire (and God
may be pleased to grant it me) that I might die in the Pulpit'.
Though 'much wasted' (Walton) by his exertions on that
Friday, Donne did not die mid-sermon. He retired to the
deanery, where, a couple of weeks later, he staged yet another
tableau in his ongoing duel with death. He had a carpenter
create a wooden platform carved in the shape of a funeral urn;
behind this he had placed a wooden board about the height
of his own body. A 'choice Painter' was hired, and several
charcoal fires made up in Donne's study. The Dean appeared,
winding sheet in hand:

> and, having put off all his cloaths, had this sheet put on him,
> and so tyed with knots at his head and feet, and his hands so
> placed, as dead bodies are usually fitted to be shrowded and
> put into their Coffin, or grave. Upon this *Vrn* he thus stood
> with his eyes shut, and with so much of the sheet turned aside
> as might shew his lean, pale, and death-like face, which was
> purposely turned toward the East, from whence he expected
> the second coming of his and our Saviour Jesus. In this posture

> he was drawn at his just height; and when the Picture was
> fully finished, he caused it to be set by his bed-side, where it
> continued, and became his hourly object till his death.

This life-sized picture of his own body arrayed in the winding
sheet that he would shortly be needing, not only served Donne
as a uniquely personal *memento mori*, but as the model for the
frontispiece that adorned *Deaths Duell* (by Martin Droeshout),
and for the upright marble statue of the poet in his grave
clothes which Henry King commissioned after his death. This
extraordinary sculpture by Nicholas Stone lay forgotten in an
obscure nook for 150 years after the Great Fire of London, but
was recovered and re-erected in 1818 in St Paul's Cathedral,
where it can be viewed today.

    Like his statue, Donne's writings have disappeared
from view for long periods of history. The eighteenth century
had very little time for him. Samuel Johnson repudiated the
far-fetched imagery of Donne and his followers as 'violent
and unnatural', and even Pope's mellifluous re-writings of a
couple of Donne satires did little for his reputation. In the
romantic era he was admired, though with certain reservations,
by Coleridge, who, like Pope, suggested ways in which the
earlier poet's rugged metrics and rebarbative diction might be
smoothed and improved. But it was not until the young T.S.
Eliot set about overhauling the canon of English poetry as
established by Francis Palgrave (who included no poems at all
by Donne in the first edition of his *Golden Treasury*[1]) that what
Johnson had called 'metaphysical' poetry suddenly became
compulsory reading for the aspiring poet or critic: 'A thought

---

[1] The volume does contain a lyric beginning 'Absence, hear thou this protestation' given
as by Anon. in 1861 but attributed to John Donne in the 1891 edition. However, the
poem is probably by John Hoskins.

to Donne was an experience; it modified his sensibility…'
This famous, though in many ways baffling, dictum ushered
in Eliot's sweeping diagnosis of the 'dissociation of sensibility'
that 'set in' in the latter half of the seventeenth century, like
a new kind of disease, and 'from which', he laments, 'we have
never recovered'. In Eliot's early quatrain poem, 'Whispers of
Immortality', Donne is figured as bracingly in touch with the
fundamentals of life and death, a paradigm of the undissociated
sensibility:

> Donne, I suppose, was such another
> Who found no substitute for sense,
> To seize and clutch and penetrate;
> Expert beyond experience,
>
> He knew the anguish of the marrow
> The ague of the skeleton;
> No contact possible to flesh
> Allayed the fever of the bone.

Donne's poems often set about conjugating the way we
experience what Eliot calls 'sense': 'Licence my roaving
hands,' he exults in 'To his Mistris Going to Bed', 'and let
them go / Before, behind, above, between, below. / Oh my
America! my new-found-land'. Even here though, the lover's
roving hands are part of a larger metaphor or conceit, one
that equates permission to explore his mistress's body with
charters granted to companies to take possession of newly
annexed territories in the New World. Indeed throughout his
oeuvre Donne's brilliant anatomies of desire rigorously resist
the illusion that the body can be presented unmediated – as
John Dryden, for one, complained:

> He Affects the Metaphysicks, not only in his Satires, but in his
> Amorous Verses, where Nature only shou'd reign; and perplexes
> the Minds of the Fair Sex with nice Speculations of Philosophy,
> when he shou'd engage their hearts, and entertain them with
> the softnesses of Love.

But nature is never allowed to reign in Donne:

> Full nakedness! All joyes are due to thee,
> As souls unbodied, bodies uncloth'd must be,
> To taste whole joyes.

Unbodying the soul at death, unclothing the body for sex: this is what Eliot defined as 'amalgamating disparate experience'.

Donne's obsessive and life-long interest in defining the precise nature of the relationship between the body and the soul, both during life and after death, is the focus of Ramie Targoff's probing and illuminating study of his poetry, letters, sermons, and religious writings. Donne has not fared particularly well with literary critics over the last couple of decades. In his compelling and influential study of 1981, *John Donne: Life, Mind and Art,* John Carey portrayed Donne the man as a ruthlessly self-serving egotist: having betrayed his faith (he was born into a well-connected Catholic family) for the sake of worldly ambition, Donne, in Carey's reading, found himself haunted by his apostasy; and while the self-division this caused played a significant role in fomenting his dazzling rhetorical ingenuity, Carey never allows us to forget for long the origins of the imaginative power of Donne's writing in his *mauvaise foi* – rather as Satan can only make his great speeches in the opening books of *Paradise Lost* because he has betrayed God and been cast into hell. The following decade Stanley Fish brought a more withering indictment still: 'Donne is sick and his poetry is sick... Donne is bulimic, someone who gorges himself to a point beyond satiety, and then sticks his finger down his throat and throws up'. The poems are read by Fish as violent fantasies of 'control and domination', in particular of the hapless girl at whom Donne directs his barrage of arguments, leaving her 'ploughed, appropriated, violated'. Like Carey, Fish concedes the unique intensity of the experience Donne's work offers, the 'masculine perswasive force' of his language, but suggests he is better approached diagnostically as a case history than as the author of poems that might move or amuse or stimulate the mind in rewarding ways.

Targoff is not particularly concerned to relate her own investigations into Donne's theological beliefs to the history of Donne criticism. Her book is refreshingly free of point-scoring off other critics, and she wastes no time in the business of justifying her approach in relation to this or that strand of contemporary theory. Her introduction persuasively makes the case for the importance of the body-soul relationship to an understanding of Donne's writings in all genres, and briskly outlines the various perspectives on this vital issue current in the period. There were mortalists who were convinced that the soul died with the body and that both were resurrected simultaneously at the Day of Judgement, and, at the other extreme, there were believers in metempsychosis who thought souls were transferred on death into another being – an idea Donne has much fun with in his grotesque and hilarious unfinished long poem, *The Progresse of the Soul*, which traces the migration of a 'deathless soul' through a mandrake, a sparrow, a couple of fish, a whale, a mouse, two wolves, and a 'gamesome' ape, who is about to consummate his love for one of the daughters of Adam, Siphatecia, when her brother surprises the unequal pair, and kills the unfortunate simian with a stone. The soul's last recorded residence in the poem is in Themech, another daughter of Adam and Eve, whom the soul enters while she's still in her mother's womb.

The knockabout comedy of this wonderfully adept and vivacious piece suggests Donne never took metempsychosis too seriously, but he did devote much thought to the puzzling dilemma of when exactly the soul entered the body, and how. There were two dominant schools of thought on this issue, Targoff explains, one known as traducianism, which held that the soul derived from one's parents, like any other organ, and was somehow imparted in the act of propagation, while the other, known as infusionism, argued that God individually infused a soul into each foetus at some point before it was born as a baby. In a letter of 1607 to his close friend Sir Henry Goodyer, Donne minutely rehearsed the flaws inherent in both hypotheses: for traducianism, he points out, makes it hard to see how the soul might have any 'naturall immortality', whereas the infusion theory leads one to question the beneficence of God, who is pictured endlessly forcing, against their will, sinless souls into corrupt, fallen bodies – 'the soul is forced to take this infection, and comes not into the body of her own disposition'. Traducianism leaves the supposedly divine soul dangerously undifferentiated from the 'matter' of the rest of our flesh, while infusionism involves God in the dubious practice of contaminating pure souls by stuffing them into inherently sinful bodies.

Still more dizzying are Donne's attempts to envisage the task awaiting the Creator when the last trump eventually blows. For Donne fervently believed that he, and all the saved, would be reunited on resurrection day with their earthly bodies, down to the very last particle. His disquisitions on this theme have an especially personal charge:

> *Ego*, I, I the same body, and the same soul, shall be recompact
> again, and be identically, numerically, individually the same
> man. The same integrity of body, and soul, and the same
> integrity in the Organs of my body, and in the faculties of my
> soul too; I shall be all there, my body, and my soul, and all my
> body, and all my soul.

The ardent literalism of such a passage points up an anxiety
about fragmentation and separation that runs like a leitmotif
though Donne's writings. How, he wonders again and again,
will God reassemble all the different bits of all the different
people who have died over the centuries?

> Where be all the splinters of that bone, which a shot have
> shivered and scattered in the Ayre? Where be all the Atoms of
> that flesh, which a *Corrasive* have eat away, or a *Consumption* hath
> breath'd, and exhal'd away from our arms, and other Limbs?
> In what wrinkle, in what furrow, in what bowel of the earth,
> ly all the graines of the ashes of a body burnt a thousand years
> since? In what corner, in what ventricle of the sea, lies all the
> jelly of a Body drowned in the *generall flood*? What coherence,
> what sympathy, what dependence maintaines any relation, any
> correspondence, between that arm that was lost in Europe,
> and that legge that was lost in Afrique or Asia, scores of yeers
> between?

This is from a sermon that Donne preached, with ghoulish
inappropriateness, at the wedding of the Earl of Bridgewater's
daughter in 1627. Our decaying corpses produce worms,
he goes on, and these worms eat us and then die, dry out,

moulder into dust, and this dust is blown into a river, and that river water enters the sea, where it 'ebbs and flows in infinite revolutions, and still, still God knows in what *Cabinet* every *seed-Pearle* lies, in what part of the world every graine of every man's dust lies'. The great day come, nothing daunted by the dispersals Donne has itemized in such unnerving detail, God 'beckens for the bodies of his Saints, and in the twinckling of an eye, that body that was scattered over all the elements, is sate down at the right hand of God, in a glorious resurrection'.

Atop his urn then, swathed in his winding sheet, Donne was rehearsing not his fast approaching earthly demise — he died some two weeks later — but the moment of his resurrection, or more precisely, Targoff suggests, the moment just *before* his resurrection. For unlike the figures in all other resurrection monuments of the period, Donne has his eyes closed, as he does in the frontispiece, and as he did while posing for the choice painter: the moment is at hand, but has not quite arrived, body and soul have been reunited, but he has not yet ascended, and Targoff compares his savouring of this moment, just before the grand climax, to his savouring at the end of 'To his Mistris Going to Bed' the moment just before his lover discards a different kind of 'white lynnen' shift:

> As liberally, as to a Midwife shewe
> Thy self: cast all, yea this white lynnen hence,
> There is no penance, much less innocence.
> To teach thee, I am naked first; why then
> What needst thou have more covering than a man.

Critics have long pointed out the continuities between the imaginative patterns developed in Donne's religious and his secular poetry. Theological issues recur regularly in the *Songs and Sonnets*, while the *Divine Poems* often make disconcerting use of sexual imagery: at the end of 'Show me deare Christ', for example, he figures the Church as at its best when it's like an all-accommodating prostitute and open to all comers ('Who is most trew, and pleasing to thee, then / When she'is embrac'd and open to most men'); and the ploughing, appropriating, and violating that Fish discerns in the love poems turns from active to passive in a Holy Sonnet like 'Batter my heart, three person'd God':

>   for I
> Except you'enthrall mee, never shall be free,
> Nor ever chast, except you ravish mee.

Targoff is particularly interested in the way the separation at death between body and soul that Donne so dreaded relates to his many poems about the separation of lovers; it was Donne who coined the word 'valediction', and his various 'Valediction' poems, but many others also, make copious use of the soul / body distinction as a way of insisting on the superlative nature of the bond between the lovers, and as a consolation for a forthcoming departure. The opening stanzas of 'A Valediction: forbidding mourning' directly compare the approaching separation of the speaker and his beloved to the moment the soul leaves the body:

> As virtuous men passe mildly away
>   And whisper to their soules, to goe,
> Whilst some of their sad friends doe say,
>   The breath goes now, and some say, no.
>
> So let us melt, and make no noise,
>   No teare-floods, nor sigh-tempests move…

The word *melt* may contain a reference to alchemy, in which Donne was much interested, for alchemy was also a means of inquiring into the way the physical and the spiritual could be first sifted apart, and then re-unified in a rarefied form. The lovers, Targoff argues, are being asked to behave like gold in an alchemical experiment that would have involved separating elements, refining them, and then recombining them; and, at the level of poetic alchemy, the word may have served as the catalyst for Donne's vision of the lovers' souls as still joined, despite his departure:

> Our two soules therefore, which are one,
>   Though I must goe, endure not yet
> A breach, but an expansion,
>   Like gold to ayery thinnesse beate.

The frequency with which Donne stages scenes of separation suggests the drama of leave-taking had a particular fascination for him; 'So, so, breake off this last lamenting kisse, / Which sucks two soules, and vapors Both away...'; 'Since she must go, and I must mourn, come night, / Environ me with darkness, whilst I write...'; 'Sweetest love, I do not goe, / For wearinesse of thee...' It was a conventional enough topos for a lyric poet, but Donne's farewell scenes are charged with an ingenuity and urgency unmatched in the work of other poets of his time. Their power and resonance are related by Targoff to a deep-seated worry about 'securing future continuity in the face of present rupture'. The challenges to that 'future continuity', however, derive not so much from the fact that he must go on a trip somewhere, as from a pervasive sense of the instability and fickleness not only of his lover – Donne's poetry is full of abrasive denunciations of unfaithful women

– but of himself too.

It is partly because his poems are so self-consciously performative that it is futile to try to derive from them a stable set of beliefs; Donne makes use of ideas and images rather as the soul in *The Progresse of the Soul* migrates through its various incumbents. At times his jousting about constancy turns nasty, as at the end of 'Communitie', where he declares:

> Chang'd loves are but chang'd sorts of meat,
> And when hee hath the kernell eate,
>   Who doth not fling away the shell?

Change is the prevailing condition that Donne's poems both enact and anatomize. Yet it's also in response to the constantly looming threat of dispersal and dissipation that he occasionally fashions static tableaux, such as that of the entranced lovers of 'The Extasie', who are presented as an unmoving icon of constancy, their hands 'firmely cimented / With a fast balme', their 'eye-beames twisted' as if their eyes were threaded 'upon one double string'. While their bodies 'like sepulchrall statues' lie on the violet-strewn bank, their souls engage in a series of dense and abstruse metaphysical arguments about souls and bodies, though these eventually result in a decision to return to the realm of the physical:

> So must pure lovers soules descend
>   T'affections, and to faculties,
> Which sense may reach and apprehend,
>   Else a great Prince in prison lies.
> To'our bodies turne wee then…

Many of Donne's most arresting lines are those presenting an image or moment frozen in defiance of the 'generall flood' of time and change:

> When my grave is broke up againe
> Some second ghest to entertaine,
> (For graves have learn'd that woman-head
> To be to more then one a Bed)
> And he that digs it, spies
> A bracelet of bright haire about the bone...

The lovers of 'The Relique', we learn, have come up with this 'device' as a way of enjoying a short reunion on resurrection day; the woman will have to visit his grave to retrieve the strands of her hair that he wears as a bracelet, so she can be physically 'recompact' before her ascension into heaven. The poet's hope is that the gravedigger who had been about to bury another corpse on top of his will take pity, and leave him to await the day of judgement undisturbed. As so often in Donne, it is the weird fusion of a complex, indeed outlandish train of reasoning with a jaggedly particular concrete image that delivers such an unexpected shock to the nervous system. Bony arm and still-shining hair are somehow both dead and alive at once. And it is the same distinctively Donnean mixture of the animate and the inanimate, of the physical and the conceptual, of the implausible and the rational, of self and other, of the intimate and the cosmic, that drives his most famous image of lovers united, in fantasy at least, in body and soul:

If they be two, they are two so
   As stiffe twin compasses are two,
Thy soule the fixt foot, makes no show
   To move, but doth, if the'other doe.

And though it in the center sit,
   Yet when the other far doth rome,
It leanes, and hearkens after it,
   And growes erect, as that comes home.

New York Review of Books (2009)

Review of *John Donne: Body and Soul* by Ramie Targoff (University of Chicago Press)

Walt Whitman's Democratic Vistas

In August of 1867 Thomas Carlyle published one of his most virulent diatribes against *Swarmery*, by which he meant the trend towards democracy. The immediate inspiration for 'Shooting Niagara: and After?' was the threat of Disraeli's Reform Act, which would double the number of adult males entitled to vote, and thus, as Carlyle saw it, unleash untold 'new supplies of blockheadism, gullibility, bribeability, [and] amenability to beer and balderdash': look at America, the beleaguered Sage of Chelsea argued, and its absurd late Civil War, prompted by what Carlyle derisively called 'the Nigger Question':

> Essentially the Nigger Question was one of the smallest; and in itself did not much concern mankind in the present time of struggles and hurries. One always rather likes the Nigger; evidently a poor blockhead with good dispositions, with affections, attachments, – with a turn for Nigger Melodies and the like: – he is the only Savage of all the coloured races that doesn't die out on sight of the White Man; but can actually live beside him, and work and increase and be merry. The Almighty Maker has appointed him to be a Servant. Under penalty of Heaven's curse, neither party to this pre-appointment shall neglect or misdo his duties therein.

Nevertheless, blinded by *Swarmery* and harried by frantic Abolitionists, the country foolishly went to war on the issue, with drastic results:

> A continent of the earth has been submerged, for certain years, by deluges as from the Pit of Hell; half a million (some say a whole million, but surely they exaggerate) of excellent White Men, full of gifts and faculty, have slit one another into horrid death, in a temporary humour, which will leave centuries of remembrance fierce enough: and three million Blacks, men and brothers (of a sort), are completely 'emancipated'; launched into the career of improvement, – likely to be 'improved off the face of the earth' in a generation or two!

In this last prophetic image Carlyle is evoking a relatively widespread evolutionary theory of the time; this held that the entire race of liberated black Americans would inevitably be wiped out in their struggle for survival with their white competitors. It was only their divinely appointed servitude that had enabled them to prosper and multiply as they had on the plantations of the South.

Carlyle's article appeared not only in the magazine *Macmillan's* in Britain, where its incendiary rhetoric caused an immediate furore, but in various American papers. Walt Whitman read it in the *New York Tribune* of 16 August. 'Carlyle always stirs me to the deeps', Whitman observed late in life in a conversation with Horace Traubel, and within a month of his perusal of Carlyle's scornful denunciations of the futility of the Civil War and his mockery of American ideals of democracy, he was planning a response. He contacted the Charles brothers, editors of the recently founded *Galaxy* magazine, offering them 'a rejoinder' to Carlyle's 'Shooting Niagara', as well as a poem initially called 'Ethiopia Commenting', but eventually retitled 'Ethiopia Saluting the Colors'. This poem is unusual in the context of Whitman's oeuvre after 1860 in its direct treatment of the issue that dominated Reconstruction America: race.

'Ethiopia Saluting the Colors' is also unusual in being in rather formal tercets, and in being spoken not by Whitman's all-embracing poetic persona, but by a specific character in the course of a specific historical event; its narrator is a soldier in the Union Army during Sherman's campaign in the Carolinas in the closing stages of the war. Most of Sherman's soldiers did not see the Civil War as about freeing slaves, but as about preserving the Union; being from the West, they had previously met few black people, and were dismayed to find their lines encumbered by thousands of emancipated slaves whom they treated, in the main, with disdain and cruelty. The historian Joseph Glatthaar sums up their prevailing attitude with this quote from one of Sherman's soldiers: 'Fight for the nigger! I'd see 'em in de bottom of a swamp before I'd fight for 'em'. Whitman's speaker is far less crude than this, but clearly appealed as a vehicle through which the poet could express his own deep uncertainties about the consequences of emancipation at the time of the poem's composition, 1867: 'Who are you dusky woman', the soldier asks,

> so ancient hardly human,
> With your woolly-white and turban'd head, and bare bony feet?
> Why rising by the roadside here, do you the colors greet?

The old woman replies in the poem's middle stanza, in italics:

> *Me master years a hundred since from my parents sunder'd,*
> *A little child, they caught me as the savage beast is caught,*
> *Then hither me across the sea the cruel slaver brought.*

These lines remind us of the extraordinary delicacy and compassion and vividness with which Whitman described the pursuit and capture of a 'hounded slave' in 'Song of Myself', ('I am the hounded slave…. I wince at the bite of the dogs, / Hell and despair are upon me….'), but the poem abruptly forecloses on this direct identification with a victim of the slave trade – 'No further does she say' – and turns to ponder a troubling gulf between the 'hardly human' woman, whose saluting of the colours implies a willingness to take a greater role in the nation's affairs, and the soldier who, although he has played his part in liberating her, seems unsure why:

> What is it fateful woman, so blear, hardly human?
> Why wag your head with turban bound, yellow, red and green?
> Are the things so strange and marvelous you see or have seen?

It is probably the only moment in Whitman's poetic corpus where he sounds almost like Thomas Hardy.

    'Strange' Whitman certainly seems to have found the effects of the Fourteenth and Fifteenth Amendments to the Constitution, which included, among other civil rights, extending the vote to black men; but nothing he wrote suggests he found these developments 'marvelous' in the modern sense of the term. Washington DC, where Whitman had been resident since 1863, was in the forefront of the experiment in enlarging the franchise, and the poet's occasional comments on the way this was reshaping the city imply his sympathies lay largely with the white citizens who were vigorously opposing the Republican drive towards a more multiracial society: of a black parade to celebrate the election of the Republican Sayles Jenks Bowen as Washington's mayor he observed in a letter to his mother:

the men were all armed with clubs or pistols – besides the
procession in the street, there was a string went along the
sidewalk in single file with bludgeons & sticks, yelling &
gesticulating like madmen – it was quite comical, yet very
disgusting & alarming in some respects – They were very
insolent, & altogether it was a strange sight – they looked like
so many wild brutes let loose...

A recently discovered manuscript indicates he was not immune
to the arguments of 'ethnological scientists' either: 'the blacks
must either filter through in time or gradually eliminate &
disappear, which is most likely though that termination is
far off, or else must so develop in mental and moral qualities
and in all the attributes of a leading and dominant race,
(which I do not think likely)'. That he hated the institution
of slavery there is no doubt: in a footnote to *Democratic Vistas*
he compares 'the extirpation of the Slaveholding Class' to
the cutting out and throwing away of a cancerous tumor.
But about black suffrage he was less sure; though he talks,
again in a footnote to *Democratic Vistas*, about favoring 'the
widest opening of the doors', it was in part his doubts about
the matter that led to the collapse of his relationship with one
of his earliest and most fervent champions, W.D. O'Connor,
author of the first extended defence of Whitman, *The Good
Gray Poet* (1866). And when Horace Traubel inquired, in 1888,
about Whitman's views on racial integration, he was dismayed
to receive the following answer: 'The nigger, like the Injun,
will be eliminated: it is the law of history, races, what-not:
always so far inexorable – always to be. Someone proves that
a superior grade of rats comes and then all the minor rats are
cleared out'.

That such views on race were at odds with his
egalitarian poetic persona was fully apparent to Whitman, and

in his post-Civil War published writings he largely skirts the issue – though in an essay of 1874 he did opine that blacks had 'about as much intellect and calibre (in the mass) as so many baboons'. One can be thankful that this offensive sentence was excised when he came to reprint the essay. In his early thirties he had strongly opposed the principle of the Fugitive Slave Act of 1850 (though he'd also argued that runaway slaves should be returned to their owners), and his sympathetic treatment of the slave on the run in 'Song of Myself' of 1855 is one of the poem's most moving encounters:

> Through the swung half-door of the kitchen I saw him
>> limpsey and weak,
> And went where he sat on a log, and led him in and
>> assured him,
> And brought water and filled a tub for his sweated body
>> and bruised feet,
> And gave him a room that entered from my own, and gave
>> him some coarse clean clothes,
> And remember perfectly well his revolving eyes and
>> his awkwardness,
> And remember putting plasters on the galls of his neck
>> and ankles;
> He stayed with me a week before he was recuperated and
>> passed north,
> I had him sit next me at table ... my firelock leaned in
>> the corner.

Whitman's racial politics have come under increasing scrutiny in recent years. They were the subject of a superb essay by Ed Folsom called 'Lucifer and Ethiopia' that was published in the collection *A Historical Guide to Walt Whitman* (edited by

David K. Reynolds (2000)), and they feature largely in his excellent introduction to this facsimile edition of the first book publication of *Democratic Vistas*. Spurred into prose by Carlyle's taunts and barbs, Whitman set himself the task of composing three essays that would defend America and Democracy, indeed would use, as he puts it in the first essay, 'America and Democracy as convertible terms'. The poetry he had written up to this point, and which he was sure would eventually lead to his being absorbed by his country as affectionately as he had absorbed it, had been inspired by the same nationalist ideal, but the unbounded faith and hope of the early editions of *Leaves of Grass* had somewhat curdled by 1867, as he confronted, and promised not to 'gloss over', 'the appalling dangers of universal suffrage in the United States'. Still, the three essays, 'Democracy', 'Personalism', and 'Orbic Literature' were intended not only to outline the challenges facing the democratic ideal in the new era, but to propose a solution, that solution being the creation of a literary culture commensurate with the new nation's achievements and potential.

For in this, for all its military and industrial and political triumphs, America had singularly failed:

> Do you call those genteel little creatures American poets? Do
> you term that perpetual, pistareen, paste-pot work, American
> art, American drama, taste, verse? I think I hear, echoed as from
> some mountain-top afar in the West, the scornful laugh of the
> Genius of These States.

As with each of the new editions of *Leaves of Grass*, the fourth of which was published shortly before he began work on 'Democracy', Whitman had high hopes that this new articulation of his vision would get him recognized as worthy the admiration, rather than the scorn, of the Genius of These States. Alas, neither the essays, only two of which eventually appeared in the *Galaxy*, nor *Democratic Vistas* itself, gained much attention outside Whitman's immediate circle, though it would become popular in Britain in a cheap edition published in 1887 by one of his socialist admirers, Ernest Rhys.

'The priest departs, the divine Literatus comes'. Whitman's conception of the role of the poet in relation to nineteenth-century American culture contrasts vividly with the indifference with which his own productions were received, even those most lavishly praised in numerous 'anonymous' reviews, which were all of course penned by Whitman himself. Nevertheless, his belief in America's overriding need for a new kind of poetry in order to fulfill the promises inherent in democracy never wavered, and it burns brightly, at times, indeed, desperately in *Democratic Vistas*. The Civil War had driven him to contemplate the possible fragmentation of the Union, a prospect he found nigh on intolerable. No 'foreign conquerors', he is confident, could subdue America, 'but the fear of conflicting and irreconcilable interiors, and the lack of a common skeleton, knitting all close, continually haunts me'. His analysis of America's cultural health is more sombre here than his poetry would ever permit, and at times verges on the savage, or Carlylean. 'Society', he writes, 'in These States, is cankered, crude, superstitious, and rotten':

> Never was there, perhaps, more hollowness at heart than at present, and here in the United States. Genuine belief seems to have left us ... The spectacle is appalling. We live in an atmosphere of hypocrisy throughout.

Terrible things happen in Whitman's poetry, as in the 'hounded slave' vignette mentioned earlier, but the poet himself remains buoyant, so he can offer solace the better: 'O despairer, here is my neck, / By God! you shall not go down! Hang your whole weight upon me'. But in *Democratic Vistas* it is Whitman himself who often seems close to despair:

> Confess that everywhere, in shop, street, church, theatre, bar-room, official chair, are pervading flippancy and vulgarity, low cunning, infidelity – everywhere, the youth puny, impudent, foppish, prematurely ripe – everywhere an abnormal libidinousness, unhealthy forms, male, female, painted, padded, dyed, chignoned, muddy complexions, bad blood, the capacity for good motherhood deceasing or deceased, shallow notions of beauty, with a range of manners, or lack of manners, (considering the advantages enjoyed,) probably the meanest to be seen in the world.

Every which way he turns he finds 'corruption, bribery, falsehood, mal-administration', and a political class consisting mainly of 'thieves and scalliwags'. It is a 'dry and flat Sahara' that Whitman surveys, one populated by 'petty grotesques, malformations, phantoms, playing meaningless antics'.

But all this the divine Literatus can cure by infusing the country with soul, with moral conscience, by modelling, as Whitman had done with such spectacular freedom and success in 'Song of Myself', the ideal democrat. Yet whereas the poems in the 1855 *Leaves of Grass* celebrate the present, defiantly and dramatically asserting that there 'will never be any more perfection than there is now', in *Democratic Vistas* Whitman must avert his gaze from the rampant materialism and tainted politics of the Reconstruction era, and peer into the future, if he is to recover his confidence in the American experiment. 'For our New World', he concedes in the book's second paragraph, 'I consider far less important for what it has done, or what it is, than for results to come'.

This faith in the future is what most distinguishes Whitman from such as Carlyle and Arnold and Ruskin, who all trace and lament an irreversible degradation in standards. Like all his publications, *Democratic Vistas* is a declaration of independence; it repudiates, as the great Preface to the 1855 edition of *Leaves of Grass* had done before it, the outdated and inappropriate literary models America had inherited from 'feudal' Europe, but to which it still appeared perversely wedded, and asks for a 'great original literature' to develop in its stead. It is only, Whitman argues, through a nation's arts that it can achieve genuine 'status', and thereby export its political system to all those other nations of the world that are so badly in need of it. At moments in *Democratic Vistas* Whitman can seem not that far from any American president of the last fifty years justifying his country's invasion of this or that rogue nation that has not yet signed up to the 'Democratic principle', a principle Whitman prophetically imagines coming, 'with imperial power', to 'dominate mankind', and then, having 'swayed the ages with a breadth and rectitude tallying Nature's own', eventually creating 'a New Earth and a New Man'.

This Utopian vision of the universal export of the American way seemed, however, a long way off in 1867; healing the rift in the Union, and what to do with all the freed slaves – these were the problems confronting President Andrew Johnson (1865-69), in whose District Attorney's office Whitman toiled by day as a government clerk, and whose leniency to the former Confederates he defended in arguments with friends such as O'Connor by night. Like Lincoln and Harriet Beecher

Stowe, Whitman had for a time been convinced that all those emancipated should be repatriated to Africa, which may be why he stresses the Ethiopian origins and African colours, yellow, red and green, of the turban of the ancient slave who catches the attention of Sherman's soldier in 'Ethiopia Saluting the Colors'.

In the end the *Galaxy* never published 'Ethiopia Saluting the Colors', perhaps because, as Folsom argues, in none of the three essays that Whitman sent the Church brothers did he get around to discussing the racial issues that the poem broaches, and which he promised not to 'gloss over'. They rejected the last essay, 'Orbic Literature' too, although Whitman assured them it was guaranteed to 'rouse editorial & critical remark'. A couple of years later, however, he had the good fortune to be taken up by the New York publisher J.S. Redfield, who in the 1850s had issued the first complete edition of the works of Edgar Allan Poe. After a decade out of publishing Redfield was looking to establish a new list, and decided the controversial Whitman should be its centre-piece. Accordingly, in late 1870 (though the title pages of all three bore the date 1871), he issued simultaneously the fifth edition of *Leaves of Grass*, *A Passage to India*, and *Democratic Vistas*. The last of these garnered some appreciative reviews across the Atlantic, but only one in the great Democracy itself: *The New York Times* dismissed it as 'one of the curiosities of the book world'. Two years later Redfield went bankrupt.

An anonymous reviewer of the 1881 edition of *Leaves of Grass* pointed out what he called 'the great anomaly of Whitman's case': here stood the poet, as in the famous frontispiece to the 1855 edition, in his slouch hat, one hand on his hip, the other in his pocket, the 'aggressive champion of democracy and the working man'; and yet his admirers, the reviewer noted, 'have been almost exclusively of a class the furthest possibly removed from that which labors for daily bread by manual work. Whitman has always been truly caviare to the multitude'. Beloved of European intellectuals, embraced by European socialist movements, treated, towards the end of his life, by his disciples as if he were almost a Messiah, his books yet remained unbought by the great American reading public, whose shelves groaned instead under tomes such as Henry Wadsworth Longfellow's *Evangeline* or *The Song of Hiawatha*. Whitman knew his work required a different kind of reader, and in *Democratic Vistas* he declared that the books of the divine Literatus were premised 'on the assumption that the process of reading is not a half-sleep, but, in highest sense, an exercise, a gymnast's struggle; that the reader is to do something for himself, must be on the alert, must himself or herself construct indeed the poem, argument, history, metaphysical essay – the text furnishing the hints, the clue, the start or framework'. Only this vigorous engagement on the reader's part will create 'a nation of supple and athletic minds, well-trained, intuitive, used to depend on themselves'. The rewards for such an engagement could hardly be greater, as so many of his poems prove; for to each of these supple, athletic, intuitive readers Whitman whispers, 'I have loved many women and men, but I love none better than you'.

London Review of Books (2011)

Review of *Democratic Vistas* by Walt Whitman (The Original Edition in Facsimile edited by Ed Folsom, University of Iowa Press)

The Double Vision of Baudelaire

Figuring oneself as Hamlet in the middle of the nineteenth century was an inherently perilous business. Think of Mr Wopsle, who performs the role in a hilariously bad production in Dickens's *Great Expectations*. When Wopsle as Hamlet wonders agonizingly about whether 'tis nobler in the mind to suffer the slings etc., he is assailed by contradictory cries from the audience: 'Some roared yes, and some no, and some inclining to both opinions said "Toss up for it"; and quite a Debating Society arose'. On seizing one of the Players' recorders in his altercation with Guildenstern, Wopsle/ Hamlet is raucously and unanimously entreated to play Rule Britannia. And when, his moralizing over, he dusts his fingers on a white napkin after handing back Yorrick's skull to the gravedigger, an inspired prankster yells out 'Wai-ter'.

Charles Baudelaire (1821-1867) had, it might well be argued, a more authentic claim to the inky cloak and cosmic melancholy of the troubled prince than any other writer of the era. His much-loved father Joseph-François Baudelaire died when Charles was only five, and for a blissful year or so he had his mother entirely to himself: 'I lived constantly through you, you were mine alone', he recalled of this period in one of his many, many painfully needy and caustically reproachful letters to his mother; 'You were both an idol and a comrade'. This symbiotic, paradisal state was abruptly terminated by the arrival on the scene of a military man, one Lieutenant-Colonel Jacques Aupick, who would in time rise to become General Aupick. Thirteen months after Baudelaire Senior's death

Aupick impregnated his not too bitterly grieving widow, and a month before she was due to give birth they were married. The baby was stillborn. Baudelaire, who eventually came to detest his stepfather with an intensity rivalling that of Hamlet for Claudius, never forgave his mother this betrayal.

In 1841, when Baudelaire was 20, Aupick, deciding he'd had enough of the young poet's wilfulness and insolence, arranged for him to journey by sea to Calcutta, where he was to remain for a year or so. Charles's 'aberrations had caused cruel anguish to his poor mother', Aupick explained in a letter to a friend justifying this dispatch of his stepson into exile. Like Hamlet, however, Baudelaire avoided completing the trip, although no pirates were involved in his escape and return. When the ship docked at Réunion in the Indian Ocean he simply refused to go any further, exchanging, in the teeth of the entreaties of the captain, who was a friend of Aupick's, the Bengal-bound *Paquebot des mers du sud* for the Bordeaux-bound *L'Alcide*. In a letter written to Aupick the day after he was deposited back on French soil Baudelaire declared himself penniless, deprived even of essentials, but as having acquired from the voyage 'a fund of good sense'. This claim was to be pretty quickly belied by the reckless extravagance with which he shortly after set about squandering the substantial inheritance that he came into later in the year from his father's estate. But if he didn't bring back a fund of good sense, something he would never really acquire, from this aborted trip to the Orient, he undoubtedly did return with a fund of exotic imagery that would be brilliantly deployed in poem after poem in *Les Fleurs du mal*.

'To be or not to be ...' Baudelaire's only recorded attempt at suicide came in 1845 when he was 24. 'I am killing myself without *grief*', he explained in his farewell letter to the

Polonius in his life, the much-derided and put-upon Narcisse Ancelle, the Mayor of Neuilly, who had been allotted the unenviable task of administering the *conseil judiciaire* imposed by the family as the only possible means of reining in Baudelaire's compulsive spending. This legal limitation on his access to funds only partially worked, for he could still borrow. He hated this *conseil judiciaire* with all the considerable powers of hatred he could muster, railing against the humiliation of being treated like an irresponsible minor; he blamed it, and those who'd forced it on him, for the spiralling debts that he incurred and the poverty and squalor of his day to day existence, as he drifted from seedy hotel to seedy hotel, everywhere pursued by importunate creditors. But it was not these debts, he insisted to Ancelle, that were driving him to kill himself, for 'nothing is easier than to rise above such things'. It was *ennui*, or melancholy, or *spleen* that lay at the root of his decision to end it all: 'I am killing myself because I cannot live any more, because the fatigue of falling asleep and the fatigue of waking are unbearable'. Yet he couldn't help adding a reference to his mother having 'involuntarily poisoned [his] life': 'She has her *husband*; she possesses a *human being*, an affection, a friendship. I myself have only *Jeanne Lemer*' (Lemer being the alternative surname of Baudelaire's money-hungry mistress Jeanne Duval, a demi-mondaine whose mixed race led to her being called *La Vénus noire*). By accident or design, the poet's knife-thrust failed to pierce any vital organs.

But Baudelaire, despite such histrionics, was as aware as Dickens of the absurdity of aping Hamlet in the era of progress. In the early poem 'La Béatrice' he presents himself wandering through a kind of waste land, 'terrains cendreux, calcinés, sans verdure' (in Francis Scarfe's prose translation, 'ashen, vacant lots, burnt to a cinder where no green grew'), sharpening, Hamlet-like, the dagger of his thoughts on his heart. While Dickens deploys humorous exaggeration and bathos to poke fun at the pretensions of narcissistically self-absorbed young men, Baudelaire uses overblown gothic; but the result is just as coruscating. Over his head he notices a sinister cloud that turns out to contain a group of vicious demons that look like cruel, inquisitive dwarves. They gaze at him coldly awhile, and then, like Mr Wopsle's audience, begin to mock him:

'Contemplons à loisir cette caricature
Et cette ombre d'Hamlet imitant sa posture,
Le regard indécis et les cheveux au vent.'

('Let us gaze our fill on this human caricature, this shade of Hamlet imitating his poses, with his distraught gaze and unkempt hair.')

Isn't it a pity, they continue, to see this 'bon vivant, / Ce gueux, cet histrion en vacances, ce drôle' ('this epicure, this pauper, this unemployed actor, this oddfellow') trying to interest nature in his sorrow, as if crickets and streams and flowers cared a jot about his misery; and most comic of all, he's even trying to impress us demons, who invented all these 'vieilles rubriques' – translated by Scarfe as 'mumbo-jumbo' – ourselves. The supreme poet prepares to turn his princely head away from the taunts of this obscene mob, like the dandyish Baudelaire disdaining his creditors or landladies, but then pauses, for he has noticed in their midst:

La reine de mon coeur au regard nonpareil,
Qui riait avec eux de ma sombre détresse
Et leur versait parfois quelque sale caresse.

(the queen of my heart, whose eyes are beyond compare, laughing with them at my dire affliction, and giving them here and there a lewd caress.)

In such a poem Baudelaire shows himself as refined a master as Dickens of the art of merciless humiliation. Central, I think, to the genius of both is a blindness to the possibility of compromise. Flaubert put it adroitly: 'You are as unyielding as marble', he wrote to the poet on reading the 1857 edition of *Les Fleurs du mal*, 'and as penetrating as an English mist'.

In the same letter Flaubert praised Baudelaire for having found a way 'to rejuvenate Romanticism'. But this rejuvenation is also Romanticism's death-knell, its satirical, demonic parody, as 'La Béatrice' (the title a sardonic reference to Dante's ideal beloved) so vividly demonstrates; and hence it is that Baudelaire now stands, Janus-faced, on the threshold of so many discussions of modernity. It was the German critic Walter Benjamin who most persuasively argued that in both his poetry and his prose Baudelaire revealed himself as the first 'writer of modern life', adapting the title of Baudelaire's encomium on the artist Constantin Guys, 'The Painter of Modern Life', published in 1863. Indeed the influence of Benjamin's essays on critical approaches to Baudelaire is so pervasive these days that they can at times come to seem a kind of double act. In *Seeing Double: Baudelaire's Modernity* Françoise Meltzer goes so far as to present Baudelaire's writing as in crucial ways incomplete without Benjamin's interpretations of it. Her argument is an attempt to push one stage further a complex metaphor used by Benjamin in a fragment never published in his lifetime, but written around 1921-22.

In it Benjamin asks us to compare time to a photographer who photographs the essence of things. However, because 'of the nature of earthly time', only the negative of that essence is recorded on the photographic plates, which can therefore not be read by contemporaries living through the history recorded on these plates. The 'elixir', writes Benjamin, 'that might act as a developing agent is unknown'. And while Baudelaire doesn't possess this vital developing fluid, he is somehow, 'thanks to infinite mental efforts', able to read the plates. 'He alone is able to extract from the negatives of essence a presentiment of its real picture. And from this presentiment speaks the negative of essence in all his poems'. Meltzer's twist on this is to suggest that, fortunately for us, Benjamin himself *does* possess the vital fluid or elixir or developing agent that can transform Baudelaire's negatives into real pictures. In other words, Baudelaire is the photographer who can record life in negatives on photographic plates that no one, including him, can read; then Benjamin, 'with the brilliance of his own retrospective vision of the poet and his city', applies the elixir that turns 'the negatives recorded by Baudelaire into the theory of modernity'.

It's an intriguing, if frequently dizzying, line of argument, and offers a way of bringing into focus, to continue the photographic metaphor, the double image that Baudelaire's writings so often convey, a contradictoriness perhaps best summed up by Christopher Isherwood in his 1949 Preface to his translation of Baudelaire's *Journaux intimes*:

> What kind of a man wrote this book?
>
> A deeply religious man, whose blasphemies horrified the orthodox. An ex-dandy, who dressed like a condemned convict. A philosopher of love, who was ill at ease with women. A revolutionary, who despised the masses. An aristocrat, who loathed the ruling class. A minority of one. A great lyric poet.

There is no disputing the fact that Benjamin's essays played, and continue to play, a major role in the concept of Baudelaire as an 'icon of modernity', yet Baudelaire's own writings betray little enthusiasm for progress or the future: 'Poetry and progress', he observed in a withering attack on the notion that photography could ever be considered a valid art form, 'are two ambitious men that hate each other, and when they meet along a pathway one or other must give way'. But then of course it was exactly Baudelaire's anxiety about what the future might hold, and alienation from the present, and recognition that the past was irrecoverable, a paradise lost that had vanished forever, that singled him out from his contemporaries, and made his work anticipate the concerns of a later age. Baudelaire's sense of displacement drove him to undertake the 'infinite mental efforts' that would allow him to pit against each other in his poetry the antinomies that besieged him as ferociously as the dwarfish demons deriding the would-be Hamlet of 'La Béatrice'. By finding ways, consciously or unconsciously, of registering the chaos of impossibilities through which he had to make his way, like some latterday Satan (with whom he often aligned himself) breasting the buffeting currents in the void between Hell and Heaven, Baudelaire created the body of writing that Benjamin would in due course hail as the gateway to the modern condition.

If Benjamin was Baudelaire's redemptive twin, his *semblable*, his *frère*, waiting in the future to apply a magical elixir to his poetic negatives, his own literary *doppelgänger* was Edgar Allan Poe, whom he discovered in 1847, two years before Poe's death. In 1848 he published his first version of a Poe tale, and over the next decade and a half translated a significant percentage of Poe's output. What Benjamin did for Baudelaire, Baudelaire did for Poe. He instantly and strongly identified with the American's febrile or enervated aristocrats, his capricious tormentors and doomed adventurers, and developed a vision of their author as a saintly victim to the brutal, vulgar forces of American capitalism. Poe helped Baudelaire to see how the dandy might be developed into the aesthetic flâneur, compulsively indulging his refined, connoisseur's curiosity in perverse defiance of the getting and spending going on all around him. Poe's devious admixture of the squalid and the outlandish, the banal and the hallucinatory, the exquisitely patterned and the disturbingly macabre, found more than an echo in the bosom of the French poet. 'No one', he declared in a particularly purple passage in an essay on Poe's life and works,

> has spun such magical tales about the exceptions of human life and of nature, the feverish curiosities that arise in convalescent states, the dying seasons, heavy with enervating splendours, warm days, sodden with damp mists, when under the soft caress of the south wind nerves are relaxed like the strings of an instrument and the eyes run over with tears that do not come from the heart, hallucination, at first leaving room for doubt but soon following, like a book, its own line of reasoning with conviction, the absurd occupying the intelligence and governing it with its own hideous logic, hysteria usurping the throne of the will, conflict reigning between nerves and mind, and man so out of tune with himself as to express grief by laughter.

No one, in America or Europe, had responded to the unwholesome world of Poe's tales and poems with such fervid enthusiasm before. Note the emphasis on the artificial ('tears that do not come from the heart') that runs like a thread through Baudelaire's own poetry, and on the exceptional.

And that such an exceptional figure, himself the creator of exceptional characters and exceptional situations, should have been brought low by the materialist culture into which he had the misfortune to be born, chimed exactly with Baudelaire's vision of the poet as misprized and ensnared, forced, like the poet and the seabird of his famous 'L'Albatros', to endure the mockery of the ignorant and malicious:

> Exilé sur le sol au milieu des huées,
> Ses ailes de géant l'empêchent de marcher.

(exiled on earth, an object of scorn, his giant wings impede him as he walks.)

Yet Poe also showed that there could be no turning a blind eye to that culture, however inhospitable; in the story 'The Man of the Crowd' Poe's narrator decides to follow an old man whose face he glimpses in the mob streaming past the window of the London coffee-house in which he's dawdling, after recovering from a long illness. Though he tracks his quarry all night, through all manner of contrasting districts, the man's behaviour remains stubbornly incomprehensible. At times he seems to parody the purposefulness of both the eagerly consuming bourgeois, and his 'hypocrite' antagonist and opposite, the aesthetically consuming flâneur: 'He entered shop after shop, priced nothing, spoke no word, and looked at all objects with a wild and vacant stare'. The narrator's attempt at the story's conclusion to allegorize the man as 'the type and genius of deep crime' registers as a singularly unconvincing attempt to evade what was becoming increasingly evident as the century progressed: the impossibility of making sense of city life.

After his return in the spring of 1842 from his one and only sea-voyage, Baudelaire only rarely stirred from Paris – until that is, in 1864, with a perversity equalling that of any of Poe's characters, he moved to Brussels, which he instantly hated, for two bitterly unhappy years that ended only when he suffered a paralytic collapse probably brought on by the syphilis he contracted in his youth. Many of the most resonant of the poems collected in the enlarged second edition of *Les Fleurs du mal* of 1861 (the earlier edition having had to be withdrawn after a ludicrous but successful prosecution for obscenity), respond to the mysteries of the city in a manner analogous to that of Poe's story:

> Fourmillante cité, cité pleine de rêves,
> Où le spectre en plein jour raccroche le passant!
> Les mystères partout coulent comme des sèves
> Dans les canaux étroits du colosse puissant.

(O swarming city, city full of dreams, where ghosts accost the passers-by in broad daylight! Mysteries flow everywhere like sap in the narrow veins of this mighty giant.)

The first two lines from 'Les Sept Vieillards' would extend the process of Franco-American literary transference, for they are cited by T.S. Eliot in his Notes to *The Waste Land* as a source for the line 'Unreal City', and by implication of the phantasmagoric aspects of the poem's London more generally. In a passage from the poem 'Le Soleil' that anticipates the urban poetics of another ardently Francophile American poet, Frank O'Hara, Baudelaire figures his traversing of the streets of Paris as an aleatory means of exploring simultaneously the city, the self, and the possibilities of poetry:

create

44

Flairant dans tous les coins les hasards de la rime,
Trébuchant sur les mots comme sur les pavés,
Heurtant parfois des vers depuis longtemps rêvés.

(scenting a chance rhyme in every corner, stumbling on words as against cobblestones, sometimes striking on verses I had long dreamt of.)

In 'The Painter of Modern Life' he compares the urban sketches of Guys with the heightened awareness of the narrator in Poe's 'The Man of the Crowd': 'The lover of universal life', he exclaims, 'moves into the crowd as though into an enormous river of electricity'. The frisson of the chance encounter is memorably captured in a poem such as 'À une passante', the subject of a fine chapter in Meltzer's study: 'La rue assourdissante autour de moi hurlait' ('The deafening street was howling round me'), it opens; amid the seething crowds he spies a woman in mourning in whose eye he glimpses the familiar *femme fatale*-ish mix of tempestuousness, gentleness, and deadly pleasure to which he is addicted. But before the poet can act she is gone – 'Un éclair … puis la nuit!' ('A flash of lightning – then darkness!') The rapidity with which erotic possibility emerges and then disappears in the poem is glossed by Benjamin as an example of 'the stigmata which life in a metropolis inflicts upon love'; a spark of enchantment followed seconds later by farewell. The image of the widowed woman – and it was during her widowhood that the young Baudelaire enjoyed his closest relationship with his mother – survives in the poem, but only as an impossibility. But it also insists on how her image continues to haunt him, as Thomas De Quincey, whom Baudelaire also translated into French, was haunted in his urban wanderings by the vanished figure of the young prostitute Ann in his *Confessions of an English Opium Eater*:

> Fugitive beauté
> Dont le regard m'a fait soudainement renaître,
> Ne te verrai-je plus que dans l'éternité?

(O vanishing beauty whose glance brought me suddenly to life again, shall I never see you once more except in eternity?)

It is not, I think, just the influence of Benjamin's image of Baudelaire as a quintessentially city poet that makes one feel that the *Tableaux parisiens* section of *Les Fleurs du mal* has worn better than the volume's many poems of doomed or vampiric love; their heady mix of sex and guilt, and tumbling hair that he bites or gets drunk on, appealed strongly to Swinburne and nineties poets such as Arthur Symons, but it's likely that most Baudelaire-readers of today prefer him out on the streets of Paris, registering the lives of the city's waifs and cast-offs, pondering its destruction at the hands of Baron Haussmann, as in the superb 'Le Cygne', or panoptically recording its furtive nightlife in a poem such as 'Le Crépuscule du soir', which opens like a film noir: 'Voici le soir charmant, ami du criminel' ('Here is the delightful evening, the criminal's friend').

The urban consciousness developed in this section of *Les Fleurs du mal* also dominates a number of the wonderful prose poems Baudelaire began writing in the second half of the 1850s, and which he sold – sometimes twice over! – to various newspapers and fugitive magazines. He intended to collect these into a volume to be called *Petits Poèmes en prose*, but it never appeared in his lifetime, probably falling victim to his somewhat unscrupulous, but never particularly successful, dealings with various different publishers. It was posthumously issued as *Le Spleen de Paris*, which is Englished by Scarfe as *Paris Blues*.

In a letter to Arsène Houssaye, whose *La Presse* published fourteen of these prose poems in 1862, Baudelaire outlined his ideal of 'a poetic prose, musical though rhythmless and rhymeless, flexible yet strong enough to identify with the lyrical impulses of the soul, the ebbs and flows of memory, the pangs of conscience'. This notion, he continues, had its origin 'in our experience of the life of great cities, the confluence and interactions of the countless relationships within them'. In one called 'Les Foules' (Crowds) he celebrates the extravagant rapture the soul enjoys when it 'yields itself entire, in all its poetry and all its charity, to the epiphany of the unforeseen, the unknown passer-by'. At such moments the random, unpredictable nature of urban experience is equated with the mysteries of divine grace. In 'Mademoiselle Bistouri' (*un bistouri* is a lancet), which describes a singular woman who obsessively hero-worships all doctors, we are enjoined to pay heed to the warped and mad lurking like 'innocent monsters' in the weird warren that is the great city. And here again he appeals to the divine – 'O Lord, have pity on the insane, the madmen and madwomen!' – eventually surmising that there can be no monsters in the eyes of God; for He knows 'comment ils *se sont faits* et comment ils auraient pu *ne pas se faire*' ('how they have made themselves into what they are, and how they could *not* have made themselves what they are').

Baudelaire may be subliminally pondering his own weirdness or monstrousness here. In an essay of 1930 T.S. Eliot argued that Baudelaire '*attached* pain to himself', and that while he had 'great strength' it was strength 'merely to *suffer*'. Certainly there is no progress to be discerned in his contorted, decades-long wrestling with the family dynamics that shaped his behaviour and character; even after Aupick's death in 1857 his relations with his mother could not be said to improve. He rarely visited her at her villa in Honfleur, where she and Aupick had retired, though his epistolary demands for money continued unabated. Baudelaire accumulated suffering as readily and compulsively as Mademoiselle Bistouri accumulates her extensive knowledge of Parisian doctors. If his double vision allowed him to imagine a God who saw how he might have escaped or transcended his misery, he lacked conclusively the elixir, to borrow Benjamin's term, needed to transform these negative intuitions into real life pictures. It was the extremity and eloquence of his response to a narrative that he could no more change than an actor can the plot of *Hamlet* that made him an exemplary precursor for writers of the next century, writers as antithetical to each other as Benjamin and Eliot. As the latter put it: 'In all his humiliating traffic with other beings, he walked secure in this high vocation, that he was capable of a damnation denied to the politicians and the newspaper editors of Paris'.

London Review of Books (2012)

Review of *Baudelaire: The Complete Verse* introduced and translated by Francis Scarfe (Anvil), *Paris Blues / Le Spleen de Paris* introduced and translated by Francis Scarfe (Anvil), and *Seeing Double: Baudelaire's Modernity* by Françoise Meltzer (University of Chicago Press)

City of Pain: The Poetry of James Thomson

In the last year of his life, James Thomson (1834–1882) composed a pair of contrasting poems on the theme of sleep. The first, 'The Sleeper', for which he was paid four guineas by the *Cornhill* magazine, where it appeared in March of 1882, describes a young woman drifting into a peaceful doze in a warm, comfortable parlour. 'The fire is in a steadfast glow', it opens

> The curtains drawn against the night;
> Upon the red couch soft and low
> Between the fire and lamp alight
> She rests half-sitting, half-reclining,
> Encompassed by the cosy shining,
> Her ruby dress with lace trimmed white.

The poet watches, fascinated, as the young woman's eyelids slowly close, and as her hand slips languidly from her chin and throat to her breast; sensual, quasi-erotic details ('The little pink-shell ear-rim flushes / With her young blood's translucent blushes, / Nestling in tresses warm as fur') are countered by an insistence on the absolute innocence of the girl and the scene: 'Her brown and blue-veined temple gleaming / Beneath the dusk of hair back-streaming / Are as a virgin's marble shrine'. He observes the effect of a dream on her sleeping features, 'fluttering o'er the lips', stirring 'the eyelids in their rest', troubling her breathing 'like a ripple on a river'. What sort of dream is she having, he wonders; the smile it evokes allows

49

him to deduce it concerns 'A pleasant not a passionate theme, / A little love, a little guile'. She doesn't, fortunately, talk in her sleep, and thus reveal to him 'the secret of some maiden feeling' he has no right to hear. The dream passes, and he watches her as she settles into 'deep sleep', 'sweet sleep', 'pure sleep from which she will awaken / Refreshed as one who hath partaken / New strength, new hope, new love, new faith'.

By the time 'The Sleeper' had appeared in the *Cornhill*, Thomson had drafted most of 'Insomnia', which he completed on 8 March, 1882 (Thomson's poetic manuscripts are all carefully dated). 'Insomnia' appeared in the first posthumous collection of Thomson's poems, *A Voice from the Nile and Other Poems*, edited by Bertram Dobell and published in 1884. It opens at midnight. Everyone else in the house where the poet is staying has gone to bed, confident of a good night's rest:

> But I with infinite weariness outworn,
> Haggard with endless nights unblessed by sleep,
> Ravaged by thoughts unutterably forlorn,
> Plunged in despairs unfathomably deep,
> Went cold and pale and trembling with affright
> Into the desert vastitude of Night,
> Arid and wild and black;
> Foreboding no oasis of sweet slumber,
> Counting beforehand all the countless number
> Of sands that are its minutes on my desolate track.

And in this foreboding he is, inevitably, proved right. While the others enjoy sleep's 'divine oblivion and repose', the poet suffers a particularly agonizing *nuit blanche*, for at the striking of each hour, a figure appears in his room. That of the hour from one to two is shrouded and sombre and has folded wings; he begs this figure, whose sex is not revealed, to unfurl them and fan slumber through his brain, only to learn that if he wants to be carried aloft on the figure's strong 'pinions' over the 'hollow night' and into morning's 'golden springs', he must fall asleep first.

This, of course, he cannot do. 'That which I ask of you', he complains, 'you ask of me' – the insomniac's Catch 22. Instead, he must cross, alone and on foot, the hour, which he figures as a deep and precipitous ravine: he must work his way down, as best he can, its steep sides, 'Staggering, stumbling, sinking depths unseen, / Shaken and bruised and gashed by stub and stone', then flounder across its furious, foaming, icy torrent-brook, and then ascend the opposite ridge, an 'awful scarp',

> Clinging to tangled root and rock-jut sharp;
> Perspiring with faint chills instead of heat,
> Trembling, and bleeding hands and knees and feet;
> Falling to rise anew;
> Until, with lamentable toil and travel
> Upon the ridge of arid sand and gravel
> I lay supine half-dead and heard the bells chime Two.

Each new 'Watcher', as he calls them, is more terrifying and implacable than the one before, and when four o'clock strikes he can bear it no longer. He dresses and leaves the house, wandering the deserted streets of the city until dawn. The immeasurable distance he feels between himself and the rest of humanity is vividly captured as the city begins to stir: 'When some stray workmen half-asleep but lusty / Passed urgent through the rainpour wild and gusty, / I felt a ghost already, planted watching there'.

One has to reach across the Channel for a term that can adequately characterize the poet of 'Insomnia' and 'The City of Dreadful Night', or poems such as 'In the Room' or 'A Real Vision of Sin' or 'To Our Ladies of Death': the Thomson of these poems is that rare thing in mid-Victorian verse, an authentic *poète maudit*, beyond consolation, condemned to record in lurid gothic 'the ghastly hours of all the timeless Hells' he lived through, and yet conscious that his words can do but feeble justice to the depths and intensity of the despair to which he was prone: 'I look back on the words already written, / And writhe by cold rage stung, by self-scorn smitten, / They are so weak and vain and infinitely inane', he observes miserably towards the end of 'Insomnia'.

Thomson's masterpiece, 'The City of Dreadful Night', was composed at more or less exactly the same time as Arthur Rimbaud's *A Season in Hell*, in the early 1870s, but rather than creating a poetic language that was '*absolument moderne*', it demonstrated — much to the profit of that great Thomson enthusiast, T.S. Eliot — how Dante's *Inferno* might serve as a model for a poet looking to describe a contemporary urban dystopia. 'Je parvins à faire s'évanouir dans mon esprit toute l'espérance humaine. Sur toute joie pour l'étrangler j'ai fait le bond sourd de la bête féroce' ('I succeeded in driving all hope from my mind. With the stealth of beasts, I leapt on every happiness and wrung its neck'), declared Rimbaud unambiguously at the opening of *A Season in Hell*. The young seer's ability to see through and cast off the belief-systems of his day resulted in the creation of an extraordinary new poetic idiom. Thomson never aspired to be a revolutionary of this kind, and his exclusion from the bourgeois comforts of hearth and home so poignantly hymned in 'The Sleeper' was involuntary and undesired, rather than deliberate and defiant.

Anne Ridler perhaps rather overstates the case when she asserts in her introduction to her 1963 edition of Thomson's poems and letters that 'it is no use looking to him for freshness of diction, for subtleties of metrical variation', but it is certainly true that Thomson delivered his unnervingly bleak vision of life after God in terms that derive, rather than secede from, his major English-language influences – Shelley, Poe and Browning.

It is this *maudit* strand in Thomson's poetry that has most often awakened the interest of later generations of readers – though, in truth, that interest has been flickering rather than constant – and that proved influential on later poets such as Eliot or, more recently, Mick Imlah, whose section on B.V. (Thomson's pen-name, short for Bysshe Vanolis [an anagram of Novalis]) in his 'Afterlives of the Poets' brilliantly recreates the poet's last days in the grip of his twin related demons, insomnia and alcohol. The part played by Thomson's dipsomania in the division between the *maudit* and the bourgeois in both his life and his work can hardly be overstated. It allies him with the split personalities depicted in various nineteenth-century explorations of the *doppelgänger,* the likes of Stevenson's Jekyll and Hyde, Poe's William Wilson, and James Hogg's Robert Wringhim in *The Private Memoirs and Confessions of a Justified Sinner.* For just as an unfathomable gulf yawns between poems such as 'The Sleeper' and its dark antithesis, 'Insomnia', or the jaunty lyrics of 'Sunday Up the River' and the unsparing 'The City of Dreadful Night', so it could sometimes seem there were two James Thomsons. A telling instance of this is related by J.W. Barrs to Thomson's first biographer, Henry Salt:

His absolute abandonment during these attacks was sufficient
to attest their nature, and no more pregnant illustration of the

metamorphosis he underwent could well be found than the remark made by his landlord's children on one such occasion. Thomson was naturally very loving with children, and children invariably returned his affection. Once, when he came back to his rooms in Huntley Street in the fullness of the change wrought by his excesses, the children went to the door to admit him, but closed it again and went to their father, telling him that 'Mr Thomson's wicked brother was at the door,' and for some time they could not recognise 'our Mr Thomson' in the figure of the dipsomaniac claiming his name.

Another friend, G.W. Foote, left this account of Thomson's alcoholism:

> He was not a toper; on the contrary, he was a remarkably temperate man, both in eating and drinking. His intemperate fits came on periodically, like other forms of madness; and naturally as he grew older and weaker they lasted longer, and the lucid intervals became shorter. The fits were invariably preceded by several days of melancholy, which deepened and deepened until intolerable. Then he flew to the alcohol, so naturally and unconsciously that when he returned to sanity he could seldom remember the circumstances of his collapse.

Foote also records Thomson once telling a friend that alcoholism ran in his family, and indeed that 'nearly all the members of it who "had brains", especially a gifted aunt of his, fell victim to its power'. Whatever its origins, Thomson's 'constitutional melencholia' (Foote's term), and the drinking sprees to which it impelled him, eventually separated him from all but the most steadfast of his friends; and it transformed London, in his imagination, into a phantasmagoric simulacrum of a city, a nocturnal urban wilderness inhabited only by ghosts and damaged, desperate exiles,

> Each adding poison to the poisoned air;
> Infections of unutterable sadness,
> Infections of unutterable madness,
> Infections of incurable despair.

'The City of Dreadful Night' stands apart from other long poems of the Victorian era that wrestle directly with theological and philosophical issues – poems such as *In Memoriam*, 'Dipsychus' or 'Empedocles on Etna' – in that, unlike Tennyson or Clough or Arnold, Thomson, by this stage of his life, had no faith to lose, and he knew it. Its introductory section states explicitly that the poem will be comprehensible only to those in a similarly faithless condition: 'pious spirits' who believe in God or hopeful 'sages who foresee a heaven on earth', Thomson trenchantly declares, 'For none of these I write, and none of these / Could read the writing if they deigned to try'. His aim, instead, is to reach out to others as metaphysically destitute as himself and let them know they're not alone, a motivation that allies the poem with numerous twentieth-century explorations of disillusionment and suffering:

> Yes, here and there some weary wanderer
>> In that same city of tremendous night,
> Will understand the speech, and feel a stir
>> Of fellowship in all-disastrous fight;
> 'I suffer mute and lonely, yet another
>> Uplifts his voice to let me know a brother
> Travels the same paths though out of sight.'
>
> (Proem, 29–35)

Compare with this, say, Philip Larkin's 'Sympathy in White Major', in which Larkin expresses the hope that his poetry will allow all those who believe they've missed out on life at least to feel part of a group of likeminded failures.

Like so much of Thomson's writing in both verse and prose, 'The City of Dreadful Night' originally appeared in the secularist magazine *The National Reformer*, edited by the militant atheist and political activist Charles Bradlaugh. Bradlaugh and Thomson first met in 1852, when both were stationed in army barracks in Ballincollig in Ireland. It was only gradually that Thomson, who had been raised an Irvingite Evangelical by his devout Scottish mother, found his beliefs being eroded not only by Bradlaugh, but by the publications of those such as Darwin and Huxley and Spenser and Lyell in the late 1850s and early 1860s. The precursor of 'The City of Dreadful Night', 'The Doom of a City' of 1857, is as lurid and, in some parts, as striking as the later poem, but in the end delivers a fairly orthodox Christian message: come the end of the world, the sinful will be punished, or at least pulverized, while an elect few will be translated to heaven, where Thomson even imagines them singing and playing harps in a 'radiant quire'. He began, however, contributing to *The National Reformer* soon after it was founded by Bradlaugh in 1860, and his numerous articles for it that decade, all signed B.V., trace an increasingly deepening scepticism that seems to have culminated in a personal crisis in 1869. On 4 November of that year he recorded in his diary: 'Burned all my old papers, manuscripts, and letters', further noting that the process took him five hours; 'But after this terrible year, I could do no less than consume the past. I can now better face the future, come in what guise it may'. No one has ever discovered exactly what made the preceding year so terrible, but shortly after this conflagration Thomson began work on the first sections of a poem that so squarely faces the future that Edmund Blunden declared it, in 1932, 'the most anticipative poem' of its time.

It consists of a Proem of six seven-line stanzas, and of 21 sections; the odd-numbered sections are written, like the Proem, in seven-line stanzas rhyming *ababccb*, while the even-numbered sections are predominantly in six-line stanzas rhyming *ababcc*, but these even-numbered sections also contain set-piece speeches by various characters composed in a range of stanza forms and rhyme schemes. As a whole the sequence is at once exquisitely shaped and beautifully varied; Thomson clearly devoted much time to the mathematical aspects of the poem, and even alerts us in a footnote to the significance of the poem's having 21 sections. He has just been describing, in Section II, how he followed the passage of a denizen of the city to three sites of traumatic significance: a church ('Here Faith died, poisoned by this charnel air'), a villa ('Here Love died, stabbed by its own worshipped pair'), and a squalid house ('Here Hope died, starved out in its utmost lair'). Like one of Dante's damned, this pilgrim seems condemned to repeat his triangular journey over and over, and when asked by the poet why, answers 'coldly' with a brilliantly effective metaphor:

> Take a watch, erase
> The signs and figures of the circling hours,
> Detach the hands, remove the dial-face;
> The works proceed until run down; although
> Bereft of purpose, void of use, still go.
> (II, 32–36)

Take a man's 70 years, Thomson then instructs us in a footnote, divide them by the 'persistent three' of dead Faith, dead Love and dead Hope, and you get this equation: $LXX \div 333 = .210$ recurring, that is the 21 sections of the poem and the 0 of the Proem repeated forever. Further, as the poet Edwin Morgan pointed out in his excellent introduction to an edition of the poem published in 1993, the triple rhyme of section I's opening stanza is deliberately repeated in section XXI's closing stanza, with one pointed, crucial difference: there / air / fair becomes air / there / despair.

In general the odd, seven-line stanza sections are devoted to meditation and description, while in the even sections Thomson presents vignettes of despair like that of the traumatized pilgrim of section II, or the character in section IV who recounts, in an idiom heavily influenced by Browning's 'Childe Roland', his journey across a nightmarish desert; he fronts its horrors boldly enough, the birds with 'savage cries and clanking wings' swooping past him, the 'fleshless fingers cold' that pluck at him, the 'Serpents, heaped pell-mell / For Devil's roll-call and some *fête* of Hell' hissing at him, until he arrives at the sea; there he meets a woman holding in her hand a red lamp that horrifyingly turns out to be her own 'burning heart' trickling blood. Appalled by this, the narrator then somehow divides himself into two: one of him stands apart and watches, while the other sinks into a swoon, and has blood dripped onto his forehead by the woman holding her lamp-heart, blood she then wipes away with her tears and hair. Eventually both swooning self and woman are washed out to sea, and the other self is left to tell his tale, Ancient Mariner-style, to anyone in the city of dreadful night who'll listen.

In their extravagance and intensity such narratives are closer to Poe, or Poe's admirer and translator, Baudelaire, than to anything in Victorian poetry, delivered though they are in a language that borrows heavily from the gothic side of Shelley and Browning. While it would take the genius of Eliot to find a way of fusing Thomson's Dantescan vision of the urban inferno with realistic details of modern London in the manner that makes *The Waste Land* so startling, Thomson's poem is not devoid of glimpses of the nocturnal city that the poet paced in the throes of his insomnia: street-lamps burn, the moonlight silvers empty squares, the dark shrouds 'countless lanes and close retreats'. While it's often signalled that the poem's city is a city of the mind ('How he arrives there none can clearly know'), at one point its silence is shattered by the 'booming and jar of ponderous wheels' and the 'trampling clash of heavy ironshod feet'; a vast dray pulled by a team of snorting horses arrives, as if we were in the middle of a bit of London scene-setting by Dickens. And the poem's river can't help but evoke the Thames:

> I sat forlornly by the river-side,
>> And watched the bridge-lamps glow like golden stars
> Above the blackness of the swelling tide,
>> Down which they struck rough gold in ruddier bars;
> And heard the heave and plashing of the flow
> Against the wall a dozen feet below.
>
> Large elm trees stood along the river-walk ...
> (VI, 1–7)

It's during his sojourn on this river-walk that he overhears a couple propound what might be described as Thomson's own brand of secularist doctrine, one that significantly lacks Bradlaugh's hope that the dissemination of atheism might relieve mankind from its mind-forged manacles and enable the creation of a better society:

> 'The world rolls round for ever like a mill;
> It grinds out death and life and good and ill;
> It has no purpose, heart or mind or will.
>
> 'While air of Space and Time's full river flow
> The mill must blindly whirl unresting so:
> It may be wearing out, but who can know?'
> (VIII, 36–41)

The most comforting thing a secularist sermonizer can find to say to a 'gloom-arrayed' congregation in section XIV is that at least loss of belief in the afterlife means that, when you eventually feel you've had enough, you can kill yourself without fear of retribution: 'But if you would not this poor life fulfil, / Lo, you are free to end it when you will, / Without the fear of waking after death' (XIV, 82-85). It was such sentiments that earned Thomson the sobriquet, bestowed by Bertram Dobell, of 'the laureate of pessimism'.

The 'anticipative' aspect of the poem is particularly strong in section XVIII, in which the protagonist wanders into a suburb in the north of the city. There he comes across a creature crawling painfully down a lane, only to realize this creature is in fact a man, or what 'had been a man', his 'Long grey unreverend locks befouled with mire'. Like so many of the maimed compulsives of Samuel Beckett's fiction and theatre, he is pursuing a hopeless quest, convinced he is on the point of discovering the 'long-lost broken golden thread' that will lead him from the unendurable present, this 'accursed night without a morn', back through 'vast wastes of horror-haunted time' to his earliest infancy, thus enabling him to revert to the state of a baby 'cradled on its mother's knee'. The unillusioned poet can only wonder at this perverse longing to 'seek oblivion through the far-off gate / Of birth, when that of death is close at hand!'

Yet, however futile the poem acknowledges all human endeavour to be, it concludes with an admiring description of a vast bronze statue erected on an 'upland bleak and bare' above the city. This statue is of the 'wingèd Woman' depicted in Albrecht Dürer's 1514 engraving *Melencolia I*. For Thomson she is a figure not only of melancholy, but also of all the ingenious means with which humanity has striven against the forces of chaos and darkness. These are precisely itemized in the poem ('a pair of compasses ... The instruments of carpentry and science ... Scales, hour-glass, bell ...'). Her wings, like those of the first Watcher in 'Insomnia', are furled, but Thomson still allows himself to derive a measure of uplift from her powers of stoical endurance in face of the naked truth of our condition (and surely he must have hoped his own poem might function in an analogous way):

> Thus has the artist copied her, and thus
> Surrounded to expound her form sublime,
> Her fate heroic and calamitous;
> Fronting the dreadful mysteries of Time,
> Unvanquished in defeat and desolation,
> Undaunted in the hopeless conflagration
> Of the day setting on her baffled prime.
> (XXI, 43–49)

Thomson goes on to commend her 'indomitable will', and even to suggest that, however 'baffled', her creativity will prove unstoppable: 'The hands shall fashion and the brain

shall pore, / And all her sorrow shall be turned to labour'.
Yet while a number of the more positive terms deployed in
high romanticism's encounters with the infinite manage to
infiltrate Thomson's vocabulary in this final section – 'sublime',
'mighty', 'passionate', 'solemn' – the knowledge with which
Dürer's wingèd woman is invested is more a summation of
than a contradiction of the poem's 'anticipative' philosophical
premises. There is nothing meaningful out there:

> The sense that every struggle brings defeat
> > Because Fate holds no prize to crown success;
> That all the oracles are dumb or cheat
> > Because they have no secret to express;
> That none can pierce the vast black veil uncertain
> Because there is no light beyond the curtain;
> > That all is vanity and nothingness.
> (XXI, 64–70)

'Behind the veil, behind the veil', exclaimed Tennyson in LVI
of *In Memoriam* when confronted with the notion that life is
'futile' as well as 'frail'. Thomson sternly dismisses this specious
comfort: none can pierce the veil because there's nothing
behind it. Although the woman's ability to persist in the face
of endless defeat allows her to seem, in the opening lines of
the poem's final stanza, a late descendant of romanticism's
various figures of intellectual beauty, and even as engaged in
some kind of ambivalent dialogue with the natural sublime,
this proves momentary, indeed almost elegiac; for the poem's
conclusion firmly indicates that the only consolation that she,
and by extension art, can truly offer, is the one he promised in
the Proem, to which this circular poem is about to return us:
a sense of solidarity in suffering:

The moving moon and stars from east to west
Circle before her in the sea of air;
Shadows and gleams glide round her solemn rest.
Her subjects often gaze up to her there:
The strong to drink new strength of iron endurance,
The weak new terrors; all, renéwed assurance
And confirmation of the old despair.

(XXI, 78–84)

In his autobiography *Something of Myself* (1937) Rudyard Kipling recalls that he read Thomson's poem in his schooldays, and that it 'shook me to my unformed core'. (He in turn composed a short story, first published in 1887, called 'The City of Dreadful Night', which describes an insomniac's ramble around the streets of Lahore, and makes numerous allusions to Thomson's poem). The poem's power to shake its readers derives in no small measure from the repetitive, hypnotic rhythms in which it presents its relentless series of disillusionments and losses. Matthew Arnold, in 'Stanzas from the Grand Chartreuse' (a poem that inspired a poetic response in kind from Thomson, 'Suggested by Matthew Arnold's *Grande Chartreuse*', composed in 1855), described himself as 'Wandering between two worlds, one dead, / The other powerless to be born, / With nowhere yet to rest my head': 'The City of Dreadful Night' makes brilliant use of Dante to create a mid-Victorian limbo in which Arnold's sense of metaphysical homelessness is shared by all, and dramatically illustrated by both a diverse cast of characters, and by Thomson's wide-ranging philosophical speculations. The latter at times take us into very murky waters indeed. In Section VII, for instance, Thomson reports that 'some say' there are phantoms abroad in the city who 'mingle freely with sparse mankind'. This mingling seems to

have a sexual element, and is again 'anticipative', in this case
of Bram Stoker's vampires haunting nocturnal London in his
novel *Dracula* of 1897. Thomson's phantoms do not, however,
feed on the blood of mankind, instead appearing to be sort of
phantom-flashers:

> The phantoms have no reticence at all;
> The nudity of flesh will blush though tameless,
> The extreme nudity of bone grins shameless,
> The unsexed skeleton mocks shroud and pall.
> (VII, 11–14)

The distinction between mankind's 'nudity of flesh' which,
however unbridled the sexual appetite, can still give rise to
feelings of shame, and the 'shameless' 'nudity of bone' of
the phantoms is a dizzying one, and seems again to prefigure
some of the ways in which Eliot recast late Victorian gothic
into something more radically unsettling, as in a poem such as
'Whispers of Immortality', with its weirdly eroticized corpses:
'And breastless creatures under ground / Leaned backwards
with a lipless grin'.

And yet, however outlandish or bewildering the
poem's speculations and cast, it never seeks to break free
from its overarching formal framework or its stately poetic
diction. The liminal world it describes is movingly implicit
in this disjunction between the daring of Thomson's thought
and the conventionality of the poem's forms and language;
its full, indeed often thumping rhymes, and insistent use of
repetitions can make the poem hover somewhere between the
incantatory and the imprisoning. If the poem's city is a place
of radical homelessness, its style yet communicates an inability
to jettison the poetic conventions Thomson inherited, leaving

it effectively stranded between two worlds, to adapt Arnold's phrase, with nowhere to rest its head.

It would, however, in time find a significant and admiring readership, though six years elapsed between the appearance of the poem in four instalments in the *National Reformer* in the spring of 1874, and its publication in a volume, *The City of Dreadful Night and Other Poems*: those other poems included 'In the Room' (which is spoken by the furniture in a room in which a man has just committed suicide), 'To Our Ladies of Death' (which imagines, Hamlet-like, the dispersal of the poet's own corpse: 'One part of me shall feed a little worm, / And it a bird on which a man may feed'), as well as a number of more cheerful sequences such as the wonderful 'Sunday at Hampstead' and the frolicsome 'Sunday Up the River'. If this book didn't quite make Thomson famous, it sold well enough to make viable the publication of a second collection, *Vane's Story, Weddah and Om-El-Bonain, and Other Poems* shortly after, and then a volume of prose pieces, *Essays and Phantasies*, the following year, 1881. But the flurry of attention garnered by the appearance of these titles occurred just when the poet was beginning to lose in earnest his battle against his own melancholy, and the dreadful nights to which it drove him. It was only in these last couple of years that he managed to earn any money from his poetry, money he fast squandered: the four guineas, for instance, that he received from the *Cornhill* for 'The Sleeper' were likely to prove, Barrs wearily noted, the occasion for another 'sad, sad spree'.

Thomson's letters of contrition on recovery from such 'sprees' are often both eloquent and unsparing; to Barrs on 22 April of 1882 he confessed:

> I scarcely know how to write to you after my atrocious and
> disgusting return for the wonderful hospitality and kindness of

yourself and Miss Barrs. I can only say that I was mad. In one
fit of frenzy I have not only lost more than I yet know, and
half murdered myself (were it not for my debts I sincerely wish
it had been wholly), but justly alienated my best and firmest
friends, old and new, both in London and Leicester.

As, unfortunately for myself at least, I am left alive,
it only remains for me to endeavour my utmost by hard and
persistent struggling to repay my money debts, for my debts
of kindness can never be repaid. If I fail, as very probably I
shall fail, the failure will but irresistibly prove what I have long
thoroughly believed, that for myself and others I am much
better dead than alive.

As apologies would be worse than useless, I will
conclude by simply expressing my deep gratitude for your
astonishing undeserved goodness to myself, and my best wishes
for the welfare of you and yours.

To his credit, Barrs himself seems to have viewed Thomson's
excesses more as a malady than a weakness. In his statement
to Salt he declared: 'No mortal ever strove against an
overpowering disease more grimly than Thomson, and when
friends were to be pained by his succumbing to the mania it
was always combated and repulsed to the last moment'. Over
the years, critics and biographers have pointed to this or that
event in Thomson's life as the decisively formative catalyst of
his ruinous addiction. The death, at the age of fourteen, of
one Matilda Weller, whom he got to know in Ireland in the
early 1850s, was popular with a number of those who wrote
memoirs of the poet in the years immediately following his
death. Bradlaugh, however, was scornful of all such attempts
to attribute his friend's views and problems to this early loss,
though he did allow that in his morbid moments Thomson

THIS DIALOGUE OF ONE

was himself prone to building a 'poetical romance about her memory'.

It is perhaps also worth pointing out that many of Thomson's friends recall him as not at all a gloomy companion. 'His light feet and merry tongue', remembers Bradlaugh's daughter, Hypatia, made him, when it came to ballroom dancing, 'one of the most desirable partners'. He was popular in a wide circle of friends, regularly engaging in all sorts of outdoor activity, from boating to grouse-shooting, from tennis to horse-riding; and he was passionately fond of music, and in particular of the works of Mozart and Beethoven.

In literary matters as well as in musical ones Thomson had excellent taste, championing Blake, Whitman, Melville, and Flaubert, translating Leopardi, Heine and Gautier (having taught himself Italian, German and French), and praising Baudelaire's *Les Paradis Artificiels*. During his two decades as a literary, political and cultural journalist for a series of secularist magazines and papers, Thomson published hundreds of reviews and essays on topics ranging from 'Religion in the Rocky Mountains' (following a trip he made to Colorado in 1872 as the Secretary of the Champion Gold and Silver Mines Company) to the curse of British Philistinism ('Bumble, Bumbledom, Bumbleism' (1865)). A number of his attacks on social injustice and on the institutions of the era, in particular on the crown and on religion, became well known in Victorian free-thinking circles. The most wittily barbed of these is 'A Famous Old Jewish Firm', which figures Jah as an irascible Jewish merchant, and reads the Bible as an account of his business dealings with Abraham and Jacob and their heirs. At length, rather like Dickens's Dombey, feeling his age and the need of a successor, Jah expands the firm into Father, Son and Co., much to the displeasure of his erstwhile partners. The Co. remains a shadowy figure, but the Son, 'with that eccentricity which has ever abundantly characterized [Jah]'s proceedings' is brought up 'as a poor Jewish youth, apparently the child of a carpenter called Joseph, and his wife Mary':

> Joseph has little or no influence with the firm, and we scarcely hear of transaction done through him, but Mary had made the most profitable use of her old *liaison* with Jah, and the majority of those who do business with the firm seek her good offices, and pay her very liberal commissions. Those who do not think so highly of her influence, deal with the house chiefly through the son, and thus it has come to pass that poor Jah is virtually ousted from his own business. He and the third partner are little more than sleeping partners, while his mistress and her son manage every affair of importance.

This new business hierarchy proves instantly successful, and the product is soon being exported all around the world. Jonathan Swift, as the above makes clear, was the dominant influence on Thomson's satirical prose style, though it must be confessed he rarely achieves the devastating verbal precision and wit of Swift at his best. His versatility as a journalist was most fully tested after he finally cut all ties with Bradlaugh and *The National Reformer* in 1875, the year after it published 'The City of Dreadful Night'; Thomson found himself reduced to writing for the trade magazine *Cope's Tobacco Plant*, a Liverpool-based journal sponsored by a tobacco company. This meant channelling his literary enthusiasms through topics related, however tangentially, to the production and consumption of tobacco, a challenge to which he often rose triumphantly. Though his critical prose is not much read these days, it's nearly always shrewd and sprightly, while his more poetic prose pieces, which he called Phantasies, such as the

stately, symphonic 'A Lady of Sorrow' or 'In Our Forest of
the Past', stand comparison with the best of De Quincey (a
powerful influence on their conception and cadences) or the
more speculative, symbolic side of Poe. The Lady of Sorrow
in the former strongly resembles the figure of the wingèd
Woman at the end of 'The City of Dreadful Night', eloquently
propounding a stoical atheism ('whatever is born in Time must
decay and perish in Time'), and hymning the comforts and
release of death. At the Phantasy's end her 'thin weird voice'
dies away 'in the dense blackness subterreanean, as a star-speck
dwindles in the formless night; and the gloom, so deep and
crushing in the revelation of her voice, grows deeper still and
yet more awful in the following utter silence'.

'Dense blackness ... formless night ... gloom ... utter
silence...': if it was Thomson's pessimism that lay behind his
appeal to such as the young Kipling and the adolescent Eliot,
the 'less deceived' aspect of his work was, in many ways,
thrust upon him, rather than being the result of a determined
questing after the new. His drinking put the tempting
comforts of bourgeois life beyond his reach, and converted
him from a poet one might ally with Coventry Patmore into
one who anticipated the despairs and disjunctions of a later
century. Given the fact that Thomson often worked in the
British Library, how tempting it is to imagine him in May
of 1873 sitting across from the eighteen-year old Rimbaud
(readers were supposed to be over 21 but the *enfant terrible*
had brazenly lied on his application for a reader's pass), both
furiously scribbling away at their nightmarish long poems.
Like *A Season in Hell*, 'The City of Dreadful Night' articulates
a radical isolation and disconnection that marks a new stage in
imaginings of the modern metropolis. The first of its epigraphs
is from Dante: 'Per me si va nella città dolente' ('Through me

is the way into the city of pain'). This was probably the first line of Dante's that Eliot ever read, and Thomson's city of pain lies, like its own 'Great ruins of an unremembered past', buried somewhere beneath Eliot's 'Unreal city', the earlier poet's roaming phantoms haunting 'shadowy streets' transformed by Eliot into zombie-like commuters flowing through fog over London Bridge.

The many dreadful nights that Thomson lived through in his last drink-addled months culminated in a binge that led to a spell in prison, and then, on 1 June, to an intestinal haemorrhage from which he died two days later in University College Hospital. His last words, according to a friend who was present at his death, were too desperate ever to be repeated.

The Oxford Handbook of Victorian Poetry, edited by Matthew Bevis (2013)

Saint Emily

Until quite recently, paper played a crucial role in the composition, and transmission to posterity, of most poems in English; they were written down on paper, or antecedents such as parchment or vellum, or typed on it, and then printed in pamphlets, newspapers, magazines or books. Computers and digitization have changed all that; the PoemHunter.com version of 'La Belle Dame Sans Merci' that floats on our screens may reproduce exactly the same words as printed editions of Keats, but while reading it we are no longer engaging with a material object that is linked to a series of earlier material versions of the poem, all deriving from the impact of pencil, pen, or type, on paper.

Digitization has also, however, inspired all manner of new approaches to materiality, which over the last two decades has developed into a boom subject in academic criticism; at the click of a mouse one can access the various different holograph versions of, say, Emily Dickinson's 'Safe in their alabaster chambers', one of the ten poems of the nearly 1,800 that she wrote which found its way into print in her lifetime. Dickinson's fragile manuscripts, which are divided between the Houghton Library at Harvard and the Archives and Special Collections of Amherst College, can be consulted and handled by only a select band of Dickinson editors and scholars; the Dickinson Electronic Archives website allows a virtual simulation of these elect scholars' and editors' experience, and encourages us to think of print editions of Dickinson's work by such as Thomas H. Johnson (1955) or R.W. Franklin

(1998) as fundamentally flawed. Over twenty years ago Jerome McGann argued that any print version of a Dickinson poem, however copious its list of variants, 'alters the original scriptural version in drastic ways'. We ought to treat, McGann insisted in *Black Riders: The Visible Language of Modernism* (1993), all of Dickinson's 'scriptural forms as potentially significant *at the aesthetic or expressive level*' [his italics]:

> Some of her scripts are highly ornamental, some are not, and we must attend to these variant features of the texts. In the same way, we have to read closely the lineation patterns, and the spacing of the scripts at every level, as well as the choice of papers and other writing materials. In a poetry that has imagined and executed itself as a scriptural rather than a typographical event, all these matters fall under the work's initial horizon of finality.

'Finality', of course, is just what such a scrupulous and attentive reader of Dickinson must at all costs avoid attempting to achieve, instead allowing all the manuscript variants and 'scriptural forms' to interact and percolate in provisional ways that do justice to Dickinson's concept of poetry as 'possibility', which, as all Dickinson readers know, is 'A fairer House than Prose – / More numerous of Windows – / Superior – for Doors –'

The drive towards seeing the manuscripts as opening the only valid windows and doors onto the authentically Dickinsonian has been made possible by state-of-the-art technology, but there also lurk, at its core, deeply atavistic motivations. Consider the terms in which Marta Werner, one of the major pioneers of the pro-manuscript movement and one of the editors of this sumptuous volume of Dickinson's 'envelope writings', describes her handling of A 821, a 25-word fragment (if one excludes a stray 'of' and a stray 'I') pencilled on the inside of a cast-off envelope, with a separate remnant of an envelope flap pinned to it. It was first published in Johnson's edition of the letters in 1958, and runs: 'Clogged | only with | Music, like | the Wheels of | Birds [on left hand flap] Afternoon and | the West and | the gorgeous | nothings | which | compose | the | sunset | keep [on right hand flap] their high | Appoint | ment [on added triangle of envelope – with 'of' and 'I' in margin]'.

> I found it by accident, in the Amherst College Library, when
> it fell (rose?) out of an acid-free envelope. If I had not held it
> lightly in my hands, I would never have suspected the manner
> in which it was assembled ... Look at it here, flying on the page,
> vying with light.

Behold, Werner's sacramental tone urges, a saint's relic, the holy wings of an angelic songster, a fragment blessed with mystic powers, miraculously rising from the sacred site of the archive.

The complex nature of this archive was well captured by Millicent Todd Bingham in her introduction to *Bolts of Melody* (1945), a selection of more than 600 poems culled from the vast trove of papers then in her possession; these had been handed over by Dickinson's sister Lavinia to Bingham's mother, Mabel Loomis Todd, who was the poet's first editor, and are the portion of Dickinson's manuscripts now housed in Amherst. Dickinson, Bingham explains, wrote on

> backs of brown-paper bags or of discarded bills, programs,
> and invitations; on tiny scraps of stationery pinned together

[like A 821]; on leaves torn from old notebooks (one such sheet
dated '1824'); on soiled and mildewed subscription blanks, or
on department- or drug-store bargain flyers from Amherst and
surrounding towns. There are pink scraps, blue and yellow
scraps, one of them a wrapper of *Chocolat Meunier*; poems
on the reverse of recipes in her own writing, on household
shopping lists, on the cut-off margins of newspapers, and on the
inside of their brown-paper wrapping.

What's more, most of the poems on these 'scraps', as they became
known for a while in Dickinson studies, 'were smothered with
alternative words and phrases crowded into every available
space – around the edges, upside down, wedged between the
lines'. Like her mother before her, Bingham decisively chose
to ignore all variants, to regularize spellings and punctuation,
and to impose titles.

The fact that Dickinson never herself prepared her
work for publication in accordance with the conventions of
her contemporary print culture has meant that her poetry
has always been uniquely vulnerable to being issued in
forms determined by the prevailing publishing, cultural and
academic orthodoxies of the day. Johnson's 1955 edition is
now routinely taken to embody the ideals and blindnesses of
the New Critical star under which it was compiled, while the
'choosing not choosing', to borrow the title of an influential
book on Dickinson's manuscripts by Sharon Cameron, that
is entailed by commitment to the variant-strewn manuscripts
brings Dickinson's work into line with the currently preferred
postmodernist template of provisionality and deferred
meaning. As Lena Christensen points out in her excellent
Editing Emily Dickinson of 2008, to edit Dickinson is to offer a
critical reading of Dickinson, and that reading will inevitably

be shaped by the preoccupations of the editor-critic's era; no doubt Susan Howe's declaration in *The Birth-mark* of 1993, the same year as McGann's *Black Riders* was published, that Dickinson's 'manuscripts should be understood as visual productions' will at some point in the future seem as wholly of its time as Todd's and Bingham's blithe imposition of titles and removal of dashes.

A volume such as *The Gorgeous Nothings* (a somewhat ironic title given the fact that the book weighs over three and a half pounds) is evidence of the wind still bellying the sails of the manuscript movement. It presents superb photographic reproductions, both front and back, of 52 (one for each week of the year?) of Dickinson's 'envelope writings', a term somewhat more dignified and purposeful than Bingham's 'scraps'. This focus on poems, or drafts of poems, composed only on envelopes fulfils McGann's injunction to pay attention to Dickinson's choice of paper, and in her introduction Jen Bervin comments on the fact that all these writings are in pencil, a pencil, she goes on to surmise, that Dickinson may well have kept in the pocket of her famous white dress. For Dickinson's 'one surviving dress has a large external pocket on the right side, where her hand would fall easily at rest'. The 'economy', Bervin continues, 'of the pocket is worth considering. An envelope is a pocket. An envelope refolds discreetly, privately, even after it has been sliced completely open'. Pictured below her introduction is a life-size image of the two-inch stub of pencil that Dickinson sent to Samuel Bowles, the editor of *The Springfield Republican* (in which 'Safe in their alabaster chambers' was published anonymously under the title 'The Sleeping'). Behold again — a trinity of relics is being staged for our contemplation: the pocket-envelope of the Dickinson dress, in which her hand would rest; the discarded envelope, prepared carefully for the moment of inscription, or indeed transfiguration, now archived and haloed in glory; and the sacred stub of pencil, kept in the fabric pocket-envelope, ready for the moment when inspiration strikes, and the no-longer-resting hand makes its all-transforming marks on the paper pocket-envelope that the poet is thriftily recycling.

Reading an author's manuscripts inevitably prompts thoughts of the original scene of writing – in Dickinson's case of the imposing Homestead in Amherst, of her bedroom there, of her diminutive writing desk (eighteen inches square), of her stitching together the booklets of poems that Todd christened fascicles, of her talking to visitors through doors, or appearing unexpectedly, like a wraith, holding a white flower ... In other words we enter the gothic world of Dickinson legend that has proved so enduring and alluring. And while treating a Dickinson holograph as an artwork can certainly make for sophisticated analysis of the 'scriptural forms' that print can never reproduce, it can also on occasion licence a disturbing degree of hagiography, and engender some unnervingly purple critical prose. Susan Howe, doyenne of the manuscript movement, figures Dickinson in the Preface to this book as a quasi-Christ figure, on the threshold of transcending the limits of mortal words but refusing to reveal that she has achieved the impossible, an enigma forever eluding our grasp, one who communicates by hitherto unknown means:

> Is there an unwritable unknown poem that exceeds anything the technique of writing can do? We will never know. Maybe this is her triumph. She has taken her secret to the grave and will not give up the ghost.
>
> To arrive as if by telepathic electricity and connect without connectives.

Clearly engagement with her manuscripts can make Dickinson devotees as light-headed as the speaker of 'I taste a liquor never brewed', who is figured as an 'Inebriate of Air' and 'Debauchee of Dew'; materiality here tends to inspire writing that strains in the opposite direction, towards the mystical or transcendental, towards a vague but uplifting 'vying with light': 'see the little Tippler / Leaning against the – Sun –'

51 of the 52 poem-envelopes reproduced in this exceptionally handsome volume come from the Amherst College Library, and only one from Harvard. The division of Dickinson's papers between these two institutions was the final act in a long and complex war fought first between two women, and then between their daughters: on one side was Mabel Loomis Todd, succeeded on her death by Millicent Todd Bingham; on the other was the wife of Dickinson's older brother Austin, Sue Dickinson, née Gilbert, who in turn passed on the feud to her only surviving child (of three), Martha Dickinson Bianchi. The current manuscript versus print battle can thus be seen as only the latest in an on-going series of conflicts over Dickinson's writings, and the ways in which they should be presented to the public – although for the early combatants far more than the matter of how Dickinson should be punctuated was at stake. For the irrepressible Mabel Loomis Todd might be said not only to have taken illegal possession of a large portion of Emily Dickinson's papers, but to have taken illegal possession of Dickinson's brother Austin, with whom she embarked on a passionate 12-year affair in 1883, more or less under the nose of his wife, Susan Dickinson. Austin and Sue lived in The Evergreens, next door to Emily and Dickinson's sister Lavinia in The Homestead; the dining room of The Homestead became one of Austin and Mabel's favourite locations for their adulterous liaisons,

although, according to Lyndall Gordon, who tells the whole story in lurid, gripping detail in her *Lives Like Loaded Guns: Emily Dickinson and Her Family's Feuds* (2010), they proved adept at finding a range of love nests in Amherst, and even, or so their diaries suggest, took to experimenting with group sex. As soon as Emily was no longer alive to prevent it, Austin made over to the Todds a plot of land on which they built a thirteen-room house called The Dell, where Austin, Mabel, and her husband David Peck Todd, established what seems to have been a largely harmonious *ménage à trois*.

Mabel, much to her chagrin, never managed to meet the elusive poet face to face, although she claimed Dickinson enjoyed hearing her play the piano, and she received from her a number of gnomic, but indubitably barbed, notes. Still, when Lavinia found herself uncertain as to what she should do with the vast mass of papers and stitched-together booklets of poems that she'd found on her sister's death, she turned for help to Todd, who was brisk, efficient, indeed brazen, and had some experience of the world of publishing. Todd at once set about creating printer's copies of the batches of poems Lavinia brought over by the basketful to The Dell; she enlisted as co-editor the influential man-of-letters T.W. Higginson, whose opinion of her work Dickinson had sought back in 1862, but to whom she had insisted the idea of publishing was as 'foreign to my thought, as Firmament to Fin'. 116 poems were agreed upon, and Todd selected as a cover a painting of her own of Indian Pipes (a white fungal plant of 'stillness, shadows and secrecy' that she claimed was both appropriate and one of the poet's favourite flowers). In November of 1890 Dickinson's *Poems* was launched on the world and sold, much to the surprise of its publishers, the Boston firm of Roberts Brothers, spectacularly well, having to be reprinted 11 times over the next year.

Would Dickinson's work have entered the public domain had Todd and her philandering husband not arrived in Amherst in late August of 1881, and been received at The Evergreens a month or so later by Amherst's leading hostess, Susan Dickinson, and her venerable husband, Austin, known, like his father before him, as 'the Squire'? Austin was fifty-four when he embarked on an affair as transgressive and unconventional as his sister's poetry – in which, incidentally, he never expressed the slightest interest – while Mabel was twenty-seven. The sheer unlikeliness of the events that led to the moment when Mabel Todd, the implacable foe of the poet's cherished sister-in-law, and the lover of her hitherto utterly respectable brother, a distinguished lawyer and the treasurer of Amherst College, contemplated her own picture of Indian Pipes on the cover of the first volume of Emily Dickinson's poems ever to be published, which she had edited, calls to mind the Dickinson line 'Not probable – the barest Chance'. Did Todd detect, one wonders, a pun in the last word of the poem she titled 'Mine', and put first in a section called 'Love': 'Mine – long as Ages steal!'

And yet, without this cuckoo's invasion of both The Evergreens and The Homestead, and the Dickinson land on which The Dell was built, it is not at all certain that Dickinson would ever have been published, or her manuscripts preserved. It's certainly a wonder that what Bingham called the 'scraps' were deemed worth keeping by her sister and her first editor. The scribbled-on, scissored-up portions of envelope so lavishly and lovingly reproduced in *The Gorgeous Nothings* were – apart from the Harvard envelope flap – among the papers brought over by Lavinia for Todd's perusal in the decade between Dickinson's death in 1886 and Lavinia's decisive rupture with Todd in 1896, a rupture occasioned by a dispute over a strip of land that Lavinia legally gifted to the Todds, only to claim later that she had been hoodwinked by Mabel and her legal witness into signing the deed of transfer. Austin, besotted to the end (he died in 1895), frequently pressured his sister to bequeath half of the copyright in Dickinson's work to Todd in recompense for her very considerable editorial labours, but Vinnie (as she was known) stoutly refused. During the decade of Todd's and Vinnie's cooperation, two further collections of Dickinson poems were published, in 1891 and 1896, as well as a two-volume edition of letters. Susan Dickinson, meanwhile, though in possession of comparable manuscript riches, made few attempts to bring her sister-in-law's work to the attention of the public, even after Vinnie died in 1899 and she inherited the manuscripts that had not been passed on to Todd. Her side entered the publishing fray only in 1914, the year after Susan herself died, with *The Single Hound*, a volume compiled from Susan's cache of Dickinson material by her daughter Martha Dickinson Bianchi. To Bianchi's credit, *The Single Hound* was the first volume not to impose titles. By this stage, however, interest in Dickinson had largely waned, and in the first decades of the twentieth century she figured little in anyone's tally of America's poetic achievements.

In the wake of her bitter legal battle with Vinnie, which she lost, Todd did not return the manuscripts entrusted to her care. She locked them in a Chinese camphorwood chest, which she placed in a barn in Amherst; and there it remained for nearly three decades – perhaps that's why some of the scraps got soiled and mildewed – while the Todds themselves decamped to Coconut Grove in Florida. Not until 1924 did Mabel and Millicent think to retrieve it, goaded this time into action by Bianchi's publication that year of *The Life and Letters of Emily Dickinson* and *The Complete Poems of Emily Dickinson*, a title of which their trove, they knew, made a mockery. The chest contained, they were pleased to discover, ammunition enough to restart the war of the houses, and for the next twenty years the sides hurled at each other both slanderous insults and Dickinsonian 'bolts of melody'. The volume of that title of 1945 was where thirty-five of the poems composed on these envelopes were first published; six had made the cut for one or other of Todd's 1890s selections, and a handful of others had to wait until Johnson's *Letters* of 1958 to appear; the Harvard fragment contributes two lines to a poem first published in *The Single Hound*.

By the 1950s, when Johnson was at work on the first scholarly edition of Dickinson's poems and her canonical status was assured, the battle to acquire Dickinson's manuscripts had reached fever pitch. Bingham was put under intense pressure to allow the collection she had 'inherited', though her legal claim to it was surely somewhat dubious, to join the rest of Dickinson's papers at Harvard; but having, as she felt, been ill-used by those now taking control of the Dickinson estate, she decided to hand them over, in 1956, to Amherst College instead. The previous year Johnson's three-volume variorum edition had appeared, its texts based for the Todd-owned portion of Dickinson's oeuvre only on photostats. For a few decades this authoritative print version made Dickinson's manuscripts appear, like those of any other poet, as interesting drafts of work that achieved its destiny when carefully edited and published in a printed book, but R. W. Franklin's facsimile edition of 1981, *The Manuscript Books of Emily Dickinson*, opened numerous Dickinson admirers' eyes to all that was elided or side-lined in a print edition of one of her poems. Franklin, ironically, would undertake the next major print edition of Dickinson's poetry, a project undermined in the view of believers in the all-importance of the manuscripts by exactly those aspects of her holographs that his pioneering facsimile edition had brought to the fore.

Old envelopes were just one of the many types of discarded paper on which Dickinson, particularly in her later, post-fascicle years, jotted down lines of poetry, so this book can offer only a sample of the vast Schwitters-style compendium of fragments that she amassed in her bedroom. The editors invite us to ponder the possibility that Dickinson razored or scissored these envelopes to make them fit for purpose in a deliberative manner, and visual indexes offer a wonderful taxonomy of envelope shapes and styles: flaps and seals, arrows, pointless arrows, envelopes with columns, envelopes with pencilled divisions, envelopes with multidirectional texts, envelopes turned diagonally … While it's likely most poets have occasionally popped this or that idea down on an old envelope that happened to come to hand, there is certainly something inherently thought-provoking in Dickinson's regular use of them for drafts of poems: 'This is my letter to the World', she observed in a poem of 1862, 'That never wrote to Me –'. In fact the world wrote to her quite a lot; one can't, indeed, overstate the importance of the postal system to Dickinson's life, and it has even been argued that the circulation of her poems through letters should be considered as in itself a form of publication, and one superior to any vulgar appearance in print, which Dickinson derided as 'the Auction / Of the Mind of Man' and a reduction of the 'Human Spirit / To Disgrace of Price –'. Dickinson's epistolary and poetic worlds overlap insistently: letters, kept safe from prying eyes by their envelopes, wing their way from one domestic space to another, and the reading of their contents can change everything: 'A great Hope fell / You heard no noise [crash] / The Ruin [havoc / damage] was within' (variants in square brackets). We will never know if a great hope really fell, and if it did what it was, but should this refer to an actual disappointment that Dickinson suffered, it's very likely that she learned the bad news by letter.

Dickinson, whose correspondence fills three volumes, wrote many letters that she never sent. The most famous of the unsent ones that survive are known as the Master Letters, a series of frankly erotic declarations of love for an older married man who has been tentatively and variously identified over the years – although some argue that he existed only as a figment of her imagination. A number of the envelopes on whose backs or insides Dickinson wrote are inscribed with the name of one of her regular correspondents – Helen Hunt, Dr J.C. Holland, his wife Mrs Holland – making one feel that for Dickinson the decision about whether or not to send a letter that she'd written could be almost as problematic as the decision about whether or not to publish the poetry that she'd written. ('What a Hazard a Letter is –' she wrote in a late fragment, 'When I think of the Hearts it has Cleft or healed I almost wince to lift my Hand to so much as a superscription'). Unseamed, opened out, filled with pencilled lines of verse, these unsent envelopes register as telling emblems of her urge to communicate, and her almost equally strong urge to withhold communication. The four stanzas of 'A great Hope fell' and 'A not admitting of the wound', (printed as one poem by Bingham and Johnson but as two by Franklin), were drafted on two such undispatched envelopes; did Dickinson relish the contrast between the enormity of the traumatic experience for which these verses seek various metaphysical or gothic metaphors, and the diminutive bits of repurposed stationery on which she wrote them out?

A not admitting of the wound
Until it grew so wide

That all my Life had entered it
And there were [was] troughs [space / room] beside –

A closing of the simple lid [Gate] that opened to the sun
Until the tender [sovreign] Carpenter [Unsuspecting
     Carpenters]
Perpetual nail it down –

There was a great deal that Dickinson needed to 'admit' before
her own simple lid was nailed down, but she knew that she
could only do so only by delivering her words obliquely –
'Tell all the truth but tell it slant – / Success in Circuit lies';
her idiosyncratic compositional habits, like her avoidance
of print and her cultivation of a coterie readership, reflect a
fundamental compulsion to maintain a 'slant' set of angles
of relation to the world; for it was only by preserving this
slantness, paradoxically, that Dickinson could maintain
unwavering faith in her poethood, and a steadfast belief that
her work, like the carriage of 'Because I could not stop for
Death', was headed 'toward Eternity –'.

    The French poet Stéphane Mallarmé composed
regularly on envelopes, but I know of only one other English-
language poet whose oeuvre includes a series of envelope
writings, or as he called them, 'pomenvylopes'. Nicholas
Moore (1918-1986) was one of the most conspicuous stars of
the London poetry scene of the 1940s, during which decade
he published seven collections and two pamphlets. For a
variety of reasons, however, Moore gave up writing at the
start of the 1950s, devoting his time instead to horticultural
pursuits such as selling seeds and landscape gardening. Alas,
when his muse finally returned on a regular basis in the 1960s,
Moore found himself decisively out of fashion; his work
was rejected by all of the poetry book and magazine editors

to whom he dispatched it, although in his twenties he had regularly appeared on both sides of the Atlantic in prestigious publications such as *Horizon*, *New Directions*, *View* and *Prairie Schooner*, and between 1945 and 1948 had no fewer than 32 poems accepted by *Poetry* (Chicago), who awarded him, in 1947, their Harriet Monroe Memorial Prize.

Moore's marginal status in the last two decades of his life, during which he nevertheless composed thousands of pages of poetry, somewhat allies him with Dickinson, although their posthumous reputations could hardly differ more extremely. The canonization of Dickinson means that even the front of a fragment of envelope gets digitally photographed and elegantly reproduced in a book such as *The Gorgeous Nothings*, because the poet happened to scribble a few lines on the back of it; Moore's vast archive of unpublished poetry was drawn upon by Peter Riley for two posthumous collections, *Lacrimae Rerum* (1988) and *Longings of the Acrobats* (1990), but for the most part sleeps undisturbed in the Cambridge University Library. Moore's few, but fervent, admirers are hoping that a fresh *Selected* that will be published later this year will revive interest in a poet whom John Ashbery has described as 'tremendously exciting and unaccountably overlooked'.

Moore's pomenvylopes are more unambiguously 'visual productions', to use Howe's phrase, than Dickinson's, and while hers seem like remote inner chambers in a labyrinth of carefully guarded privacies, Moore's could be read by whatever Royal Mail employees were involved in sorting and delivering them; Moore, that is, would type away on the back, and front, of an envelope, leaving free a small square for address and stamps; hence all involved in the missive's journey from poet to recipient might pause in their labours to peruse a meditation on what goes to make a poet ('A pen, some paper, / Maybe even a typewriter'), a poetic version of a bit of Ariston, a satirical dig at 'Big Spender' or 'El Scior Alvarez', a squib poking fun at 'The Poetry Boob Society' or 'The Darts Council'. I worked for a while as a postman – how refreshing it would have been to find amid the bills and circulars and birthday cards one of Moore's fantastically mottoed and illustrated envelopes, sporting both his own name and a variety of anagrammatic pseudonyms such as Armin Coolhose, Alonso Moriche, or Lhoso Cinaremo. And while Dickinson's are all composed in pencil, Moore's come in a cheerful array of differently coloured typewriter ribbons: turquoise, green, brown. One that was passed on to me by the publisher and writer Anthony Rudolf, a frequent recipient, offers a witty version of an epigram, once attributed to Plato, that was addressed to a boy called Aster (i.e. star); this 'translation special pomenvylope' is date-stamped 26 January 1970, the very year the Beatles broke up:

> You gaze up in the night-sky,
> Ringo, having chosen yourself to be one of the Starrs,
> And I only wish that I
> Had all those eyes to gaze back into yours.

Moore's own 'slanted' relationship to the culture in which he found himself during the late sixties and early seventies, the heyday of his pomenvylope period, is lightly gestured towards in the central pun of his neologism: for certainly a degree of envy drives Moore's rambunctious riffs on poets and rock stars and news-makers of all kinds. 'Fame,' as Dickinson observed in a late poem that neatly captures the disappointments of the second phase of Moore's poetic career, 'is a fickle food / Upon a shifting plate / Whose table once a / Guest but not / The second time is set'.

In striking contrast to the unwieldy *The Gorgeous Nothings*, the German writer Francis Nenik's *The Marvel of Biographical Bookkeeping* weighs a mere two ounces. It twins the life story of Nicholas Moore with that of the Czech poet Ivan Blatný (1919-1990), whom Nenik figures as Moore's Iron Curtain *doppelgänger*. Blatný, like Moore, had enjoyed an illustrious decade as a poet in his twenties, publishing eight volumes between 1938 and 1947. Shortly after the Communist coup of 1948 he came to London as a delegate on a cultural exchange trip funded by the British Council; on his first night in the country he announced on the BBC that he would not be returning to Czechoslovakia, and would be seeking asylum. In his home country he was denounced, declared officially dead, and his poetry banned.

Blatný worked for a while in London as a freelance journalist and writer. His mental health, however, became fragile; in 1954 he was admitted to Claybury Hospital in Essex, where he stayed until 1963. The last twenty-seven years of his life were spent in two institutions in Ipswich: House of Hope and St Clement's Hospital; in the former everything he wrote was thrown away by attendants who thought him just another lunatic nurturing delusions that he was a writer, but a nurse in the latter happened to discover in the course of a trip to Czechoslovakia that Blatný was indeed a poet of some repute. He was, accordingly, given a supply of paper, and allowed to write poetry rather than make lampshades; the nurse, one Frances Meacham, preserved his manuscripts in a bin in her garage. Like those of Dickinson stored for decades in a barn in Amherst, they too would eventually make their unlikely way into an archive, being acquired, after the Velvet Revolution, by the Museum of National Literature in Prague.

Nenik's ingenious little book is in two halves. In the first section he develops a series of parallels between Moore's and Blatný's experiences through an adaptation of the technique of double-entry bookkeeping. The verso presents the melancholy events of Moore's life, the recto Blatný's; each paragraph makes use of roughly the same syntax and they share much vocabulary, allowing their stories to overlap and intertwine. The result is a haunting lament for two voices on the perilousness of poetic election, on the random collisions and attritions and strokes of fortune that made their lives fulfil so completely those rueful lines of Wordsworth's in 'Resolution and Independence': 'We Poets in our youth begin in gladness; / But thereof come in the end despondency and madness'. Here, but in succession rather than in parallel, are the book's opening paragraphs:

> When the critic George Steiner looked through the entries for the *Sunday Times* Baudelaire translation competition he was judging in 1968, he was no doubt a little surprised. Someone had submitted more than thirty versions of the same poem.

> *When the journalist Jürgen Serke came across a slim man with a small cut on his freshly shaven cheek in St. Clements Hospital in Ipswich in 1981, he was no doubt a little surprised. The man had been declared dead more than thirty years previously.*

> That someone was Nicholas Moore, an aspiring English poet during the 1940s, who had somehow disappeared from the radar at the end of that decade and had not made a reappearance since.

> *That man was Ivan Blatný, an aspiring Czech poet during the 1940s, who had absconded from his delegation on a trip to London in 1948 and then disappeared.*

That is, Nicholas Moore had never really disappeared; instead he had slipped unnoticed into the workings of time and, in addition, had suffered a series of blows of fate, all of which he had somehow survived. Yet in the world of letters, Nicholas Moore was a dead man, catapulted out of a literary machinery revolving ever faster, and often merely around itself.

That is, Ivan Blatný had never really disappeared; instead he was struggling with paranoia as a result of his escape and exile, which took him behind the secure walls of various English hospitals. Yet in the world of letters, Ivan Blatný was a dead man, his name erased by a literary machinery surviving on suppression and silencing.

1948 was his fateful year. And it went like this:

1948 was his fateful year. And it went like this:

Distresses, disasters, weird compulsions unite their lives at every turn: Blatný is diagnosed with paranoid schizophrenia, Moore with diabetes; Blatný's poetry piles up in Frances Meacham's rubbish bin in her garage, Moore's in his chaotic flat in St Mary Cray; Blatný composes in a baffling mixture of Czech, German, French and English, while Moore makes use of a range of outlandish personae (Helga Nevvadotoomuch, Phil Okes-Box-Wunnayay, Harrowsmith Blamesworthy) and far-fetched idioms; Blatný is confined to the grounds of his asylum, Moore, after the amputation of a foot, to a wheelchair. Both narratives conclude with their respective poets pursuing their vocation to the bitter end, facing death with pen in hand: 'he is lying in a hospital bed and writing a poem'; *'he is lying in a hospital bed and writing a poem'*.

Moore and Blatný never met, and indeed probably never
even heard of each other, but this doesn't deter Nenik from
imagining for them a correspondence conducted in late 1962
and early 1963. Nenik claims, in best Borgesian fashion,
to have stumbled across these letters, which make up the
second section of *The Marvel of Biographical Bookkeeping*, in the
course of research that he undertook in 2011 in the London
Metropolitan Archives; an Author's Note even offers an
elaborate bibliographical description of the notebook of
Blatný's in which the correspondence was preserved. The
letters themselves are a touching fictional tribute to two poets
lost 'in the maze' of literary history, to adapt the last line of
'In Memoriam', one of the hundreds of poems composed
by Blatný during his time in St Clement's; despite its title
this poetic 'scrap' is so delicately slanted that it recalls not
Tennyson, nor its ostensible subject Walter de la Mare, but
Saint Emily of Amherst:

> Walter de la Mare died 1956
> the year of the hungarian uprising
> so he won't read my old-fashioned poems
>
> Was he a Londoner?
> Did he live in the country?
> Why had we to lose him in the maze.

London Review of Books (2014)

Review of *Emily Dickinson: The Gorgeous Nothings* edited by Marta Werner
and Jen Bervin (Christine Burgin / New Directions) and *The Marvel of Biographical Bookkeeping* by Francis Nenik, trans. Katy Derbyshire (Readux)

Owls, Bicycles, Bailiffs:
The Pataphysical Life of Alfred Jarry

Arthur Rimbaud, in his famous letter of 15 May, 1871, argued that a poet could only make himself into a *'seer* by a long, immense and reasoned *disordering* of *all the senses'*. The French poet, playwright and novelist Alfred Jarry couldn't have read this letter which was only published in 1912, five years after Jarry's death at the age of 34 from a mixture of tuberculosis, poverty and alcoholism, but there can be little doubt that he would have agreed with Rimbaud's assessment of what it took to become a *'seer'*.

Here is the memoirist and *femme de lettres* Rachilde's description of a typical day in the life of her friend:

> Jarry began the day by consuming two litres of white wine, then three absinthes between ten o'clock and midday, at lunch he washed down his fish, or his steak, with red or white wine alternating with further absinthes. In the afternoon, a few cups of coffee laced with brandy or other spirits whose names I've forgotten, then, with dinner – after, of course, more aperitifs – he would still be able to take at least two bottles of any vintage, good or bad. Now I never saw him really drunk …

When he couldn't afford alcohol, he imbibed ether instead. For both Rimbaud and Jarry, the aim of this systematic self-poisoning was to achieve god-like power: 'he becomes', enthused Rimbaud, 'the sickest of the sick, the great criminal, the great accursed, – and the Supreme Knower! – For he arrives at the *unknown*!' Rimbaud was only sixteen when he wrote this, and his projected life of visionary excess lay all before him. Writing towards the end of the journey, in one of his last texts, the autobiographical *La Dragonne* of 1906, Jarry presented himself assuming a somewhat different kind of godhead: 'He became like a monstrous divinity with the face of a bull, his forehead enlarged and his eyes parted'.

The word 'monster' hovers over many of the descriptions and discussions of the life of Alfred Jarry, who is surely Rimbaud's only true rival for the accolade of the most *terrible* of the many *enfants terribles* thrown up by French literature. One should at once point out that, for Jarry, to call something 'monstrous' was to praise it in the highest possible terms: 'I call "monster" every original inexhaustible beauty', he observed in an essay published when he was only twenty. His most enduring and resonant creation was the monstrous Père Ubu, who so scandalized Parisian theatre-goers that a full-scale riot broke out in the auditorium on the night *Ubu Roi* opened – and closed – at the Théâtre de l'Œuvre on 10 December, 1896; and Ubu, in all his unregenerate monstrosity, might be said to have stalked through the monstrous history of the twentieth century, a prototype for every scruple-free dictator from Stalin to Idi Amin to Colonel Gaddafi. Jarry, though by no means a political animal, unleashed in *Ubu Roi* a sort of sneak preview of the wars and tyrannies to come, and even the most unnerving scenes in the explicitly *engagé* theatre of later playwrights such as Bertolt Brecht or Edward Bond seem prefigured by Père Ubu's blasé, uninhibited greed. Consider this extract from a scene in which Ubu sets about collecting taxes from the peasants of Poland – this is after assassinating King Wenceslas and seizing power in a farcical, yet successful, coup d'état:

PA UBU. I've come to tell you, order you, and inform you that you are to produce and display your ready cash immediately, or you'll be massacred. Come on in, my lords of phynance, you sons of whores, wheel in the phynancial wheelbarrow.

The wheelbarrow is wheeled in.

STANISLAS. Sire, we are down on the register for only one hundred and fifty-two rix-dollars, which we've already paid over six weeks ago come Michaelmas.

PA UBU. That may well be so, but I've changed the government and I've had it announced in the official gazette that all the present taxes have to be paid twice over, and all those I may think up later on will have to be paid three times over. With this system, I'll soon make a fortune: then I'll kill everyone in the world, and go away.

PEASANTS. Mercy, Lord Ubu, have pity on us. We are poor, simple people.

PA UBU. I couldn't care less. Pay up.

PEASANTS. But we can't, we've already paid.

PA UBU. Fork out! Or I'll give you the works good and proper: torture, twisting of the neck, and decapitation. Hornstrumpot, am I or am I not your King?

When the peasants resist they are duly massacred, and the scene's representative 'Peasant's House' is razed to the ground. Père Ubu, a stage direction informs us, 'stays behind to scoop up the cash'.

Ubu, bizarrely – another word, like 'monstrous', that clings to discussions of the Jarryesque like a burr – began life as a schoolboy spoof of one Félix-Frédéric Hébert, a hopeless and hated Physics teacher at the *lycée* Jarry attended in Rennes. The grossly incompetent Père Hébert – also known as Heb, Eb, Ébé – had spawned an extensive cult among the *potaches*, or schoolboys, long before the diminutive but arrogant and uncompromising Jarry arrived in 1888. The Morin bothers, Charles and Henri, had already made him the protagonist of various plays, and one, *Les Polonais*, is in fact the basis for *Ubu Roi*. Jarry and the Morin brothers performed this as a puppet show, with marionettes made by Jarry's sister Charlotte, in the attic of the Morins' house – hence the subtitle to the first edition of the play of June, 1896: 'Restored in Its Entirety as It was Performed by the Marionettes of the Théâtre des Phynances in 1888.' Phynance here is a nod to Heb's, and his later incarnation Ubu's, love of money, a typical Jarry distortion. The play's notorious opening word, and one that is then frequently repeated, is another: 'Merdre!' – normally translated as 'Pschitt!'

Jarry's subtitle certainly gestures towards the collaborative origins of the play, and Alastair Brotchie, in this enthralling, scrupulously researched, and elegantly written biography, recounts in full detail the furore that erupted when a critic called Charles Chassé published a book in 1921 that attempted to debunk Jarry by exposing his infamous play as nothing more than a collective schoolboy prank. It was Jarry's genius to see how this adolescent *jeu d'esprit*, once translated to a theatre, could evolve into something revolutionary in a range of different ways. While that opening word signalled an explosive shot across the bows of the well-made play, the production's marionette-style staging and defiant anti-realism anticipated many of the developments in theatre that were later classified as 'The Absurd'. Its backdrop was painted by, among others, Pierre Bonnard, Toulouse-Lautrec, and Édouard Vuillard, and featured a hanged skeleton, a steaming chamberpot in a fireplace, and a bed covered in snow. To indicate settings Jarry decided a placard should be hung at the beginning of each scene to show where it took place. To a nervous Lugné-Poe, the Director of the Théâtre de l'Œuvre, he persuasivly argued in a letter of January 1896:

> I am absolutely convinced that a descriptive placard has far more 'suggestive' power than any stage scenery. No scenery, no array of walkers-on could really evoke 'the Polish Army marching across the Ukraine'.

This bright idea would again prove to have far-reaching consequences for the theatre of the twentieth century.

Far from being upset by the pandemonium sparked by his play, it seems Jarry played a significant role in stirring up the conflict, organizing a 'counter-*claque*', that is a posse of supporters whom he instructed to boo in the unlikely event the piece went down well, and to cheer if it received abuse. 'The performance must not be allowed to reach its conclusion', he insisted, 'the theatre must explode'. Probably the first night would have achieved the *succès de scandale* Jarry had in mind without this counter-*claque*, but his recruiting of them indicates the extent to which he craved a kind of anarchy in the auditorium to mirror that enacted in the play itself. On cue, catcalls and fistfights erupted, as Père Ubu, played by the actor Firmin Gémier, kitted out in a moustachioed mask and false belly, and brandishing a toilet brush as a sceptre, blithely revealed his rapacity and cowardice – a sort of ur-Homer Simpson rampaging through a mind-boggling, Monty Pythonesque narrative. W.B. Yeats happened to be in the audience that night, and while he cheered the play on, feeling, as he put it in his *Autobiography*, 'bound to support the more spirited party', he also acknowledged, with a tinge of melancholy, that Ubu represented the end of an era, as if Jarry had that night given birth to the 'rough beast' that 'slouches towards Bethlehem to be born' at the end of the apocalyptic 'The Second Coming' of 1919. Père Ubu, Yeats prophetically noted, was the form modernity would take: 'After us' [meaning nineteenth-century late romantics such as Mallarmé and Verlaine and himself], he noted in conclusion, 'the Savage God'.

The precocious Jarry had absorbed the work of Nietzsche while still in his *lycée* at Rennes, and Ubu can certainly be construed as one of the least comforting of *ubermenschen* indulging his will to power. More crucial, probably, was his discovery of the work of the self-styled Comte de Lautréamont, aka Isidore Ducasse, author, before his death at the age of 24, of the luridly transgressive *Les Chants de Maldoror*, whose gothic superhero at one point has sex with a shark. As Brotchie notes, some of Jarry's early work is 'grotesquely Maldororian in style', but while Maldoror's hair-raising cruelties exhibit a Sadean inventiveness and refinement, Ubu's crimes are essentially banal; in the words of Boggerlas, son of the assassinated King Wenceslas, Ubu is 'a common little adventurer, a mister nobody from nowhere, fat toad, stinking tramp'. Rabelais was Jarry's other great inspiration, and indeed he toiled for years over a libretto based on *Pantagruel* that was finally staged in 1911, four years after his death. There is an earthiness to Jarry's humour in all the many genres in which he wrote: his philosophical, or '*néo-scientifique*' novel, *Exploits and Opinions of Doctor Faustroll* (which again saw the light of day only after his death) features a bum-faced baboon called Bosse-de-Nage whose only but repeated utterance is 'Ha-ha'. The name Faustroll itself captures Jarry's determination to blend 'dissonant elements' in order to create the monstrous, to quote again from the essay he wrote when he was twenty: the cerebral, philosophical Faust is yoked to the all-too-physical troll, and it is interesting to learn from Brotchie that Jarry took the part of the Troll-King in a production of *Peer Gynt* staged by Lugné-Poe at the Œuvre in November of 1896. Lugné-Poe praised Jarry's performance as 'enooormous', though clearly he wasn't prepared for the equally 'enooormous' response to the show that succeeded *Peer Gynt* the following month. Stung by the vituperative attacks of the conservative press on *Ubu Roi*, Lugné-Poe distanced himself from the aberrant young playwright, and Jarry's involvement with live theatre – as opposed to puppets – was effectively at an end.

If Père Ubu never trod the boards again in Jarry's lifetime, he yet made continued appearances in life through Jarry himself, who assumed his creation's mannerisms and idiom, and was famous in literary circles for his uninflected staccato speech. Jarry commentators are prone to complaining about the attention given to the anecdotes and legends that swirl around their subject at the expense of his writings, but, as his French biographer Noël Arnaud noted, 'Jarry was not innocent of his myth'. One might go further and say that Jarry made it all but impossible to separate the two, or so Guillaume Apollinaire argued in an influential memoir published two years after Jarry's death: 'Alfred Jarry was a man of letters', wrote Apollinaire, 'to an unprecedented extent. His smallest actions, his childish pranks, everything he did was literature. His whole life was shaped by literature, and only by literature'.

MARK FORD

André Breton pursued this line still further, arguing that Jarry had brought the 'distinction between art and life, long considered essential [particularly to the Symbolists who nourished Jarry's own early writings]', to the verge of being 'abolished in principle'. Brotchie is wary of such readings, citing numerous testimonies from Jarry's friends that stress the gulf between his public and private personas. And Jarry's life was by no means merely a 'hoard of destructions', to quote Wallace Stevens quoting Picasso. He spent many months of each year on the banks of the Seine, where he indulged his love of boating and fishing, classic leisure activities of the bougeoisie so often mocked in his writings. Certainly he inspired deep and enduring loyalty from such as Rachilde and her husband Alfred Vallette, though their patience was often sorely tried by his Ubu-esque antics and idiom; the latter involved not only staccato delivery, but adoption of the royal we, and numerous Homeric-style epithets, the wind, for example, becoming 'celui qui souffle'. This Ubu-patois proved contagious wherever he went, for it was adopted not only by elite Parisian literary types, but also by the very unliterary *habitués* of the various cafés Jarry patronized during extended stays in the provinces.

Jarry emerges from Brotchie's skilful collaging of the evidence as a figure of tremendous charisma, and it was surely this charisma which prompted Apollinaire (with whom he shared a taste for billiards), to read his friend's life as a work of art. There is also, though, something authentically 'Pataphysical' – if that isn't an oxymoron – in such readings. Jarry defined 'Pataphysics', which, like Ubu, had its origins in the taunting of the Physics teacher Hébert back in the *lycée* at Rennes, as the 'science of imaginary solutions'; by examining 'the laws governing exceptions, [it] will explain the universe supplementary to this one'. If, pondering such definitions, one feels vertiginously adrift in a Borgesian labyrinth – well, that may be just one further indication of Jarry's power to anticipate the dilemmas that would afflict and motivate his literary descendants.

A more prosaic, or at least Darwinian, assessor of Jarry's slow 'suicide by hallucination', to use the term coined by Roger Shattuck in his brilliant study of the Belle Époque, *The Banquet Years* of 1955, might linger over the fact that his aunt was an alcoholic, who, like Jarry, wandered the streets in outlandish, threadbare clothes, and his maternal grandmother died in an insane asylum in Rennes the year of his birth. Drinking himself to death may occasionally have seemed to Jarry an exciting aesthetic programme, but it also ran in the family. His sister, Charlotte, died an alcoholic too, and in poverty, having had to sell the properties she inherited from their parents to cover the debts left by Jarry at his death.

Owls, bicycles, bailiffs, and his famous pistol, later acquired by Picasso, are dominant motifs in the Jarry legend – and fish, for, for many years, he lived off what he caught with his own rod in the Seine. (This was in the days before he gave up eating, having realized that 'drinking on an empty stomach is more efficacious'). The owls he kept in his apartment in Paris, an apartment he christened the *Calvaire du Trucidé* – the Calvary of the Slaughtered – unbothered by their droppings and chunks of raw meat festering around the room. The bicycle was his favoured mode of transport, and one of his wittiest, and most explicitly blasphemous essays, is entitled 'The Passion Considered as an Uphill Bicycle Race'. Barabbas, though slated to take part, is scratched at the last minute, while Pilate is the starter. Jesus begins promisingly, but then suffers a puncture when he cycles over some thorns, and is forced to carry his bike frame – 'or, if you will, the cross'– the rest of the way. There are fourteen turns in the treacherous Golgotha course, and Jesus finally falls at the twelfth – though only to continue the race 'airborne'.

There is much Christian iconography in many of Jarry's works, and he was particularly excited by medieval Christian woodcuts, founding two magazines, *L'Ymagier* and *Perhinderion*, in which he reproduced choice examples of these, along with Epinal prints and engravings by Dürer. This fascination with primitivism again looks forward to what would develop into one of the vital catalysts of modernism, and is reflected also in Jarry's own deliberately crude woodcuts and drawings – the most famous of which is his feral, snouty Ubu – and love of marionettes. There is no doubt that his tastes in this were shaped by his childhood years (from age five to fifteen) in Brittany, that remote and mythical region from which another precursor of modernism, Tristan Corbière, also hailed. Parallel to Jarry's vein of iconoclasm ran a vein of literalness, and one is somehow not surprised to learn that when, in May of 1906, he was convinced he was about to die, he had a priest summoned to administer extreme unction. In the event Père Ubu recovered (by this point his identity was so entangled in that of his alter ego that the letters he wrote describing this experience are in the third person and from the perspective of Ubu), staggering on through a further eighteen months of dissipation before succumbing in November of 1907. He remained unaware to the end that he was suffering from tuberculosis, which was only diagnosed at the autopsy.

In his discussion of Jarry in *The Banquet Years* Shattuck declared:

> There are virtually no standards by which to judge the role
> Jarry created and the *décors* with which he surrounded himself in

order to sustain himself. He left behind every standard, ethic, maxim, golden rule, and secret of success.

This biography does quite beautiful justice to these *décors* that have proved so essential to the Jarry cult. It is lavishly illustrated, and beautifully designed, and offers a detailed account of the precise make, dimensions, and chain (36 teeth) of Jarry's bicycle, one he ordered from a certain Jules Trochon in 1896, and was to be dunned for by Trochon's exasperated bailiffs for the rest of his life. While Jarry's oeuvre consistently evades, as Shattuck suggests, the clutches of conventional literary standards, in life he proved equally elusive to a whole series of dogged debt-collectors. Brotchie reproduces some of their letters, which were all treated in an appropriately Pataphysical manner by the sublimely irresponsible Ubu.

Still, though hard to grasp – and sections of his writing, it must be confessed, are so hermetic they make a poem by Mallarmé (a great Jarry admirer, incidentally) read like a newsflash – Jarry yet had an 'enooormous' influence on a number of key twentieth-century artists: Picasso (it is still unclear whether he and Jarry ever actually met), Marcel Duchamp, Tristan Tzara and André Breton head this list, while later admirers range from Italo Calvino to Gilles Deleuze, from Ionesco to Guy Debord, from Georges Perec to Jean Baudrillard. And while he inspired acute 'physical repulsion' in Lord Alfred Douglas (not necessarily a bad sign) when they met in 1897, Oscar Wilde was most taken with him, declaring him 'extraordinary', 'very corrupt', 'most attractive', and looking 'like a very nice renter' (London slang for a male prostitute). Wilde, it is often said, was never wrong, but here I think he does err; for it was on account of Jarry's intransigent refusal to be available for hire to anyone, at any price, that his life and works came to embody so vividly the intrinsic and ultimate Pataphysical ideal.

New York Review of Books (2012)

Review of *Alfred Jarry: A Pataphysical Life* by Alastair Brotchie (The MIT Press)

Ezra Pound's Letters Home

By my count, though I may have missed a few, this is the twenty-fifth volume of Ezra Pound's highly distinctive correspondence to see the light of day. The first selection of his letters, edited by D.D. Paige and culled from the years 1907-1941, was published back in 1950, when Pound was four years into what would be a 12-year sojourn in St Elizabeths Hospital in Washington, to which he'd been confined indefinitely after pleading insanity at his trial for treason in 1946. Paige's selection introduced to the world madcap Ez the compulsive letter-writer, all hectoring capitals and italics and doolally spelling and slash-happy punctuation, here berating recalcitrant magazine editors, there puffing his chosen (in the main, pretty *well* chosen) band of *Modernistas*; here, somewhat less happily, solving the world's political and economic woes by promoting Social Credit, there championing the achievements of his great hero, Benito Mussolini. Coming the year after the huge scandal caused by the Bollingen Committee's decision to award its annual prize to *The Pisan Cantos*, the book's publication caused something of a furore – as indeed did all things Poundian in the immediate post-war era.

A small batch of his letters to Louis Untermeyer was published a few years after Pound's release from St Elizabeths in 1958, and then, in 1967, his extensive, fascinating correspondence with James Joyce. It was not, however, until the 1980s and 1990s that the archive floodgates really opened. These decades saw the appearance of volumes individually devoted to Pound's letters not only to fellow authors such as

Wyndham Lewis, E.E. Cummings, Ford Madox Ford, Louis Zukofsky and William Carlos Williams, but also to various patrons and editors: to the somewhat mysterious Margaret Cravens, a Paris-based piano student from Madison, Indiana, who in 1910 bestowed on Pound an annual stipend so he could concentrate on his poetry, only to commit suicide two years later; to John Quinn, lawyer, and art and manuscript collector – including the manuscript of *The Waste Land*; to James Laughlin, founder and editor of New Directions (or Nude Erections as Pound like to call it); to Alice Corbin Henderson of *Poetry*; to Scofield Thayer and James Sibley Watson of the *Dial*; to Margaret Anderson of the *Little Review*. Two hefty books collected first his courtship letters to Dorothy Shakespear, and then those written to her some thirty years later from the Disciplinary Training Centre at Pisa, where he was first incarcerated after surrendering to U.S. Forces in May of 1945 – a move prompted by his fear of being summarily executed by victorious Italian partisans. And anyone yearning for yet more of EP's cracker-barrel (with the emphasis firmly on the *cracker*) views on political and economic matters could read his spirited, if somewhat over-optimistic, attempts to convert Senator Bronson Cutting, Congressman George Tinkham, and Senator William E. Borah to Poundian solutions to American policy issues; these were collected in volumes published in 1995, 1996 and 2001 respectively.

His epistolary career commenced, though, long before the starting dates of all of the above, with this of 1895 to his mother, who was visiting relatives in New York. Pound was nearly ten:

> Dear Ma,
>
>   I went to a ball game on saturday, between our school

and Heacocks, the score was thirty-five to thirty-seven our
favor, it was a hard fight in which wee were victorise.
They put on a colorerd man for first base and then to
pitcher but he soon was knoct out as he gave two ma[n]y men
baces on balls, as it didn't do any good they chucked him off, the
umpire cheated until pa came and then he quit

This cheating umpire, who, in the telling, was forced to quit
by the arrival of Pound's Pa, might be seen as the first of many
instances in Pound's writings of institutional malfeasance
needing to be confronted by the heroic, dissenting individual.
If the mild-mannered Homer Loomis Pound, who worked
nearly all his life in the same fairly humble job in the Assayer's
department at the United States Mint in Philadelphia,
beginning on a salary of $5 a day that rose, in nearly 30 years
service, to only $2,500 a year, did somehow challenge and
defeat the crooked umpire (whom the young Pound goes
on to suggest might have been bribed), this was very much
the exception rather than the rule. Pound's casually bullying
letters to his father, whom he tended to treat as his literary
factotum, suggest that in the main Homer was more than
happy to accept the role of awestruck progenitor and enabler
of genius, whatever the cost – and there are not all that many
letters home from the early part of Pound's career that don't
contain a request for funds or acknowledgement of money
received. 'Being family to a wild poet aint no bed of roses
but you stand the strain just fine', Pound compliments him
in a letter of 9 January, 1909, sent from London. The benign,
ungrudging Homer seems to have complaisantly endured
being chivvied in letter after letter to look after his impatient
son's literary interests in America by liaising with editors or
drumming up subscriptions for magazines to which Pound

contributed, or by using what contacts he had to procure favourable review coverage for his U.S. publications. Homer, it is clear, by no means provided a paternal template for the aggressive individualism that would come to mark Pound's increasingly vituperative attacks on his numerous and diverse targets, targets that would range from literary London to F.D. Roosevelt (or 'Franklin D. Frankfurter Jewsfeld' as he took to calling him), from the Victorian anthologist Palgrave to American universities, from the deeply loathed Winston Churchill to the 'kikefied usurers' – to borrow a phrase from one of his wartime radio broadcasts – whom he came to blame for both the First and Second World Wars.

This book contains 849 letters or postcards, not all of them of surpassing interest. This is from 9 January 1908, from Crawfordsville, Indiana, where Pound had recently begun work as an instructor in romance languages at Wabash College:

> Dear Mother -
> [Pound always wrote to his parents separately]
>
> I don't know that there is anything especial.
> Two lectures out of the way. I can't send 'em to Dad 'cause
> they're only notes & my improvisations & reading out of books.
> Things run smoothely. that is about all there is to be reported.
>
> Love to you and Dad
> EP

The book's editors, Mary de Rachewiltz (Pound's daughter by the American violinist Olga Rudge), and Joanna and A. David Moody (who is currently at work on a multivolume biography of Pound) have opted to include every missive from the wild poet back to his parents in its entirety, however mundane. I suppose one might pause to note from the above the extent to which Pound was open to sharing with his father his work-in-progress, even if it was only university lectures; and indeed Pound's literary successes – and those of his friends and acolytes – dominate most of these bulletins back to Mr and Mrs Pound from their only offspring. Occasionally the editors vouchsafe a glimpse of Homer's uncertain but enthusiastic responses to the increasingly rebarbative poetry his genius son sent back from storied Europe to suburban Philadelphia. On receipt of a first draft of what would end up as Canto II, the one that begins 'Hang it all, Robert Browning', Homer records that reading it made him feel 'like one going up in an Airship – The Mechanician has honored me with a seat – and we are soon up in the pure azure – Time and space are nothing …' He modestly declares his opinion of little value, but reports himself 'glad that in that little room – in London a son of mine can lose himself in such matters'. However, he rather timidly ventures:

> may I be permitted to suggest that as this poem is not for the Yahoos – for after the first word it soars way above the crowd – so use a different word than "hang" It seems to me "Listen-all" would be a better word …

After this hesitant stab at reining in his son's mild expletive, Homer confesses, rather plangently, that there are 'many words and names that I do not understand as you well know – but nevertheless it gives one a desire to see the places – I wish, some day we can go over them together –'

How revealing are these letters of the processes whereby a not particularly gifted language student from a middle-ranking university became one of the major catalysts of international modernism, and the author of the most polyglot poetry the world has yet produced? They certainly flesh out the indignities of his university career, particularly after he transferred from the University of Pennsylvania to Hamilton College, in Clinton, New York; there he was one of the few students refused entry to a fraternity house, and had to spend most of his time alone. Yet a decade or so on, and Pound had developed into the vibrant centre of an artistic circle that changed the course of both poetry and fiction as decisively as any in literary history.

'You just go on your nerve', Frank O'Hara famously declared of the business of writing poetry, and Pound developed a nerve like no other. What is so weird and unique about his poetry, however, is not just the nerve that it exhibits, whether this takes the form of mistranslating Propertius or chopping up bits of John Adams into unreadable cantos or baffling us with Chinese ideograms, but its bewilderingly complete dependence on other literary sources to get going. A tiny early poem, 'On His Own Face in a Glass', from his first collection *A Lume Spento* (1908) gestures somewhat melodramatically towards his lack of a secure sense of selfhood, filling a whole line with 'I', spaces and question marks:

I   ?   I   ?   I   ?

The poem that precedes it in *A Lume Spento*, 'Masks', suggests the only solution Pound would ever find to this extreme sense of hollowness or absence, which was one, it might well be argued, that he projected back onto his native land in his frequent denunciations of America as a cultural desert. In 'Masks' he celebrates how 'tales of old disguisings' can become 'Strange myths of souls that found themselves among / Unwonted folk that spake an hostile tongue'. By 'tales of old disguisings' he seems to mean the literary tradition that would furnish him with all his various masks or personae or hero-figures, from the swashbuckling Provençal troubadour Bertran de Born to the Renaissance man of action Sigismondo Malatesta, from the Anglo-Saxon Seafarer to the Bowmen of Shu, from the wise, unwobbling Confucius to the ever-resourceful Odysseus. Although obsessed with the importance of defining and promulgating a central poetic canon that would in due course inspire an American *Risorgimento*, Pound seems to have experienced his own poetic selfhood as radically disjointed and centreless. And this resulted in an oeuvre that has no centre, 'a tangle of works unfinished', as he put it in a very late canto, in which he goes on to acknowledge that his 'errors and wrecks' lie all about him, and that he could not 'make it cohere'. Notes for an even later one return to the dilemma staged by 'On His Own Face in the Glass' and 'Masks':

> That I lost my center
>   fighting the world.
> The dreams clash
>   and are shattered –

Some 60 years on, and the terms in which he construes the drama between the absent self and the dreams or 'tales of old disguisings' have hardly changed. The melodrama, of course, remains too, and is present in nearly all of Pound's most resonant moments: 'As a lone ant from a broken ant-hill / from the wreckage of Europe, ego scriptor'; 'Old Ez folded his blankets / Neither Eos nor Hesperus suffered wrong at my hands'.

The hints of vulnerability dramatized in 'On His Own Face in the Glass' and the late cantos and fragments are rare indeed in Pound. Even at his unhappiest, writing home from the 'wilderness' of Hamilton College, an element of bravado keeps interrupting his attempts to convey his loneliness:

> Absolute isolation from all 'humanity' does not tend to increase punctiliousness.
> Don't be alarmed, there are a few white folks even up here.
> Nice disagreeable sort of letter isn't it? Glad you & dad seem to be enjoying life.
> I don't suppose anyone can live in books steadily & not get grouched occasionaly. Have seen & heard nothing out-side this cramped narrow lopsided hole except last Saturday.
> I'm not grumbling only it gets monotonous.

His early poems abound in figures who translate this fear of monotony and isolation into a high romantic rhetoric of bravado derived largely from Robert Browning – 'Bah!' exclaims Cino, based on the troubadour Cino da Pistoia, a friend of Dante's, in another poem from *A Lume Spento*, 'I have sung women in three cities, / But it is all the same; / And I will sing of the sun'. Vagabonds and rovers, blood-red spearsmen, red-cloaked ladies in towers high, woodlands dim … Pound's early effusions failed to strike a chord with the much more savvy and sophisticated Eliot when pressed upon him by the *Harvard Advocate* editor W. G. Tinckom-Fernandez in 1909: 'It seemed to me rather fancy old-fashioned romantic stuff, cloak-and-dagger kind of stuff', he later recalled, a half-century later, in his *Paris Review* interview; 'I wasn't very impressed by it'.

Pound first visited Europe in 1898 with his mother,

Isabel, and her sister Aunt Frank, when he was 12. He was eager to relate to his father that during a trip to Kenilworth Castle 'the guide kept our party, after the others had left and showed us the dining room, where no visitors are allowed'. Pound's delight in penetrating into regions beyond the official itinerary, so striking in his own research – and interpretative – habits in later life, seems already in evidence here. The family made a second grand tour, on which Homer was included, in 1902, and this volume reprints a hilarious photo from the party's visit to the Alhambra in Granada, with Homer, Isabel, and the 16-year old Ra, as he was then still called, sporting elaborate Moorish costumes. As if in anticipation of Eliot's comment, the young Pound is kitted out with a flowing robe and sword, and cradles an enormously long antique flintlock rifle.

Looking back on these early visits to Europe, he decided – this is from a letter of 1912 to Aunt Frank – that they had saved him a great deal of 'work', by which he seems to have meant that they enabled him to absorb European culture intuitively. 'Really', he observed in a letter of 1916 to Iris Barry, 'one DON'T need to know a language. One NEEDS, damn well needs, to know the few hundred words in the few really good poems that any language has in it'. Unlike the more rigorously scholarly Eliot, who in 'Tradition and the Individual Talent' declared that proper knowledge of a tradition could only be obtained by 'great labour', Pound was, I think, it's fair to say, always something of a bluffer – and indeed late in life even allowed he'd never really read much, though I doubt the various annotators who have devoted their lives to tracking down his allusions would second this.

How different twentieth-century poetry would have been had these two bookish Americans opted for the university careers with which both flirted in their early twenties: 'found a new good poet named Eliot', Pound proclaims to Homer in a letter of 22 September 1914, and immediately set about arranging for 'The Love Song of J. Alfred Prufrock' to appear in *Poetry* (Chicago), for which he acted as 'foreign correspondent' and general browbeater of its founding editor, poor Harriet Monroe. Like so many young London literati of this period – Wyndham Lewis and T.E. Hulme and Richard Aldington and F.S. Flint – Eliot fell under the spell of Pound's beguiling mixture of flamboyance and generosity and startling self-confidence. Together they orchestrated what in hindsight can seem like virtually a hostile take over of the somewhat moribund London poetry scene. In return for his promotion and support of Eliot, which would reach its climax in his majesterial editing of *The Waste Land* – for which he'd also arrange the awarding of *The Dial*'s annual prize of $2,000 – Pound suggested the younger poet might explain to the world the crucial nature of his own poetic innovations. 'Ezra Pound: His Metric and Poetry' was published by Knopf (heavily subsidized by John Quinn) as a pamphlet in 1917, and was the first sustained critical assessment of his work. It was, however, issued anonymously, for as Pound observed in a letter to Quinn, it might otherwise seem rather too naked a bit of mutual back-scratching: 'I want to boom Eliot, and one cant have too obvious a ping-pong match at that sort of thing'.

Pound also played a major role in dissuading Eliot from returning to Harvard and the academic life probably awaiting him there, and was delighted when Eliot decided to marry Vivienne Haigh-Wood, despite her skittishness and troubling nerves, to stay in London, and to write poetry. *Il miglior fabbro*'s own renunciation of the cloistered groves of academe had occurred seven years previously, in 1908, in the course of his second semester at Wabash, and also involved an English woman, one normally described as a female impersonator (it seems she specialized in doing monocled toffs, an act for which, alas, there proved little demand in Crawfordsville). On Pound's own account, he ran into her on a street corner one freezing night, and, taking pity, generously invited her back to his lodgings to get warm. She slept in his bed, he slept on the floor, but this offence against decency, when brought to the attention of the Wabash College authorities, was enough to get him summoned by the Dean. 'Dear Dad', he wrote (c. 13 February, 1908),

> Have had a bust up, but come out with enough to take me to Europe. Home Saturday or Sunday. Don't let mother get excited.
>
> Ez
>
> I guess something that one does not see. but something very big & white back of the destinies. has the turning & the leading of things & this thing. & I breath again.

As an afterthought he added, 'In fact you need say nothing to mother till I come'. (Throughout these letters Pound is far more confiding to his father than his mother, to whom he is often somewhat testy, complaining for instance, of her 'general objection to my way of doing nearly everything'). On official investigation of the matter Pound was exonerated and offered his job back, but by then he'd decided he'd had enough of university life in a small mid-Western town. 'Dear Dad', he wrote a few days later, 'Have been recalled but think I should rather go to ze sunny Italia'. He was paid the balance of that month's salary, $200, and felt able to depart as undisputed victor in the row: 'Have had more fun out of the fracasso than there is in a dog-fight & hope I have taught 'em how to run a college'.

By late April he was installed in Venice, 'By the soap-smooth stone posts where San Vio / meets with Il Canal Grande' (Canto LXXVI). From there he writes back to his 'Benign & Reverend Parent', in answer to an inquiry into the state of his finances; 'I am by no means sure it would not be pleasanter to starve the body in Venice than to starve the soul in a backwoods hamlet'. Anyway, courtesy of remittances from home and his redundancy check, he was able to pay a Venetian printer to produce 150 copies of *A Lume Spento*, one of which he dispatched to W.B. Yeats. Yeats courteously replied that he found the book 'charming'. A more public acclamation of his talent came from the popular 'poetess' – as the review's headline describes her – Ella Wheeler Wilcox, a Pound family friend, who exclaimed in the *American Journal-Examiner*: 'Success to you, young singer in Venice! Success to '"With Tapers Quenched"'. An even more enthusiastic review appeared in the *Evening Standard & St James Gazette*, shortly after the young singer had moved to London and set about making his mark on the literary scene there: 'Wild and haunting stuff, absolutely poetic, original, imaginative, passionate, and spiritual … words are no good in describing it'. The author of this encomium, described merely as 'a Venetian critic', was almost certainly Pound himself.

Like Whitman before him, with whom he made a pact in the 1913 poem of that name, arguing they shared 'one sap and one root', and that accordingly there should be 'commerce between us', Pound devoted enormous amounts of time and energy to the business of self-promotion. Of course Whitman pinned his colours wholly to the mast of American democracy, while Pound committed himself to what, on the face of it, looked like an antithetical programme – the wholesale denunciation of American culture, which he dismissed, in a poem addressed to another American exception, the painter James McNeil Whistler, as the work of a 'mass of dolts'. Eliot took firm steps in his introduction to Pound's *Selected Poems* of 1928 to separate his maverick modernist *confrère*, to whom he still felt deeply grateful for the caesarian Pound had performed on *The Waste Land*, from the embarrassment of an association with Whitman, ignoring Pound's acknowledgement in 'A Pact' of his 'pigheaded father': 'I am ... certain' observed Eliot, in his best pulpit manner, '– it is indeed obvious – that Pound owes nothing to Whitman'. Yet the tradition of the American huckster lurks somewhere in the hinterland of both, and these letters show Pound as easily matching the shameless Whitman in acts of self-boosterism, badgering his father to prod and harry U.S. editors and reviewers, and offering in return an artlessly boastful account of his conquests in literary London: Laurence Binyon, Henry Newbolt, Maurice Hewlett, Victor Plarr, Selwyn Image, Ford Madox Ford ... and finally, after months of networking and glimpses from afar, Yeats himself! In a letter of 30 April, 1909, he records spending five hours with the Irish bard the day before, and of a change of plan: 'I shall not go to Venice. the London game seems to have too many chances in it to risk missing them by absence'. Of those Pound targeted only one significant player eluded him, as he recalled in Canto LXXXII, written in the DTC at Pisa: 'Swinburne my only miss'.

But unlike Eliot and Henry James (finally located and secured in March of 1912), Pound never sought to be absorbed into British society, though he was keen to inform his mother, in the letter recounting his meeting with James, that he was now established enough to 'revolve' in the 'strata' of London society described in James's novels. It is to her that he recounts such triumphs as a 'weekend with Lady Low in Dorset', for, proud of her Wadsworth pedigree, and a distant connection to Henry Wadsworth Longfellow, Isabel harboured hopes her gifted son might restore some of the ancestral respectability squandered by her wastrel father, whose itinerant career included a spell peddling patent medicines and toothache pellets. If only Ezra could get appointed to a post in the London American embassy! But it was the life of a bohemian that her errant son adopted in London, one subsidized first by his parents, then by Margaret Cravens, and then by his wife Dorothy's annuity of £150 a year. Not that, like his maternal grandfather Harding Weston, he didn't occasionally dream up get-rich-quick schemes, such as his proposal to William Carlos Williams that they open a syphilis clinic together on the north coast of Africa; Pound's expansive 'social proclivities' would secure a clientele of 'wealthy old nabobs' for Dr Williams to treat, and they'd be able to 'clean up a million ... and retire to our literary enjoyment within, at most, a year'.

In the poem to Whistler, first published in 1912, Pound attempted to characterize the dilemma facing the genuine American artist:

> You had your searches, your uncertainties,
> And this is good to know – for us, I mean,
> Who bear the brunt of our America
> And try to wrench her impulse into art.

Pound's self-education in Europe was never conceived by him as an escape from what was involved in being a 'murkn', to use his own orthography, but the best way of bearing the 'brunt' of what he considered his nation's inadequate culture, so as to 'wrench' it towards a significant national art. His poems are directed towards those whom he addresses in another poem on this theme, 'The Rest', as 'the helpless few in my country, / O remnant enslaved!' To this elect but thwarted tribe, in thrall to the 'mass of dolts' in the so-called land of the free, Pound's aesthetic feats in Europe will serve as both paradigm and encouragement:

> You of the finer sense,
> Broken against false knowledge,
> You who can know at first hand,
> Hated, shut in, mistrusted:
>
> Take thought:
> I have weathered the storm,
> I have beaten out my exile.

The strenuous, adversarial nature of this process meant that, like such as Thoreau in *Walden*, or Whitman in *Democratic Vistas*, or James in *The American Scene*, Pound could be seen as contributing to that most venerable of American genres, the Jeremiad; however, in leading him to embrace the antithesis of American democracy, Italian fascism, it would eventually put him decisively beyond the pale of even the generously capacious and forgiving traditions of American dissent. What's more, it led him to seek out scapegoats for the political and artistic frustrations he suffered, and from 1916 on attacks on 'chews' begin sporadically to disfigure his writings, including these letters. While he seems to have met little firm resistance from his parents in this slide towards extremism, a letter of Homer's reprinted here, in response to one of Pound's that has been lost, does record his being asked at some function, 'Why does Ezra hate the Jews?' and having to reply that he didn't know. 'Why', he continues, 'if it was not for them (the jews) here in Phila – this old town would be a desert. They are the ballast in this old ship ...' Ezra begged to differ, and while there is nothing in these missives to match the rabid rantings of his wartime radio broadcasts, in one of which he commended Hitler for 'having seen the Jew puke in the German democracy', while in another he advocated, instead of 'an old style killing of small Jews' a more targeted 'pogrom UP AT THE TOP' of 'the sixty Kikes who started this war', they still on occasion make for queasy reading. One gets the sense that his parents, for the most part, opted to sidestep these issues when his letters raised them, deeming such fulminations part and parcel of being a wild poet.

On Homer's retirement from the Mint in 1928, the Depression looming, they decided to join the son of whom they'd seen so little over the previous two decades during which he'd been beating out his exile, and settle in Rapallo, whither Pound and Dorothy had moved from Paris four years previously. They found, on arrival there in 1929, a rather more complicated situation than they'd anticipated. Shortly after the shift to Italy, Pound's mistress Olga Rudge had given birth to a daughter Mary in July of 1925, in the Italian Tyrol; the baby was almost immediately handed over to foster parents to be brought up in the mountain village of Gais. The following year Dorothy had produced a son, Omar, who had been just as summarily dispatched, first to a certain Madame Collignon who lived just outside Paris ('she has two children of her own', Dorothy assured her puzzled in-laws, 'and knows all about bottles and milk and such like'), and then to an ex-Norland nanny in Felpham, Sussex. Pound had concealed from his parents the existence of Mary, and his letter announcing the birth of Omar was elliptical in the extreme:

> Dear Dad
>> next generation (male) arrived.
>> Both D & it appear to be doing well.
>> Ford going to U.S. to lecture in October.
>> Have told him you wd. probably be glad to
>> put him up.
>> more anon,
>>> yrs
>>> E

Months later his parents were still pumping him for basic information, such as the date of Omar's birth.

Their presence in Rapallo made it hard for Pound to maintain this epistolary stonewalling. To his father he confided the secret of Mary's birth, and even took him to visit her in Gais. If Isabel was told, it seems she simply decided to ignore this distressing and inconvenient fact. It was only a decade on, however, in the summer of 1939, that his parents appear to have been offered an explanation for Pound's indifference to Omar, who was by now at Prep school in Bognor Regis. In her memoir of Isabel and Homer that prefaces this volume, Mary tactfully but unequivocally makes clear her opinion that Pound was not Omar's father, and suggests that it was the revelation of this that prompted two bewildered letters preserved in Pound's files: 'Dear Son', wrote Isabel on 31 July, 1939,

> The situation is to me amazing – one disloyalty provokes
> another is understandable but why continue the deception so
> many years one cannot transfer affections –

Three days later Homer wrote:

> My Dear Son.
> A clap of Thunder out of a clear sky could not have been more
> startling than yours and D's letters. For over 10 years we have
> been here. D. has been giving us Omar's photos ok and it is hard
> to realize the truth. Why did you suggest our remaining? As
> matters have developed there is no pleasure in our continuing
> here.
> We shall arrange to – depart –
> > Your Old
> > Dad

In the event they didn't abandon Ezra, whose behaviour
during this period was becoming increasingly erratic, and
return to America, despite making extensive preparations to
do so. Homer fractured a hip in 1941, and died the following
year, one hopes without having tuned in too frequently to the
broadcasts that would lead to his son's indictment for treason
in 1943. Isabel survived Homer by six years, eventually laying
aside 'old resentments', as Mary put it in her autobiography
Discretions (1971), and joining her granddaughter in Schloss
Neuhaus, an abandoned castle above Gais in the south Tyrol.
She died and was buried there in February of 1948.

'May you live in interesting times' … Pound's life
often brings to mind the old Chinese proverb, occasionally
attributed to Confucius, to whose teachings he increasingly
looked for world salvation during his incarceration in St
Elizabeths, where he in time gathered around him a motley
crew of would-be poets, anti-Semites and white supremacists.
It was only five years before his death, in conversation with
Allen Ginsberg in 1967, that he explicitly turned on himself

for falling prey to 'that stupid, suburban prejudice of anti-Semitism'. These letters back to 166 Fernbrook Avenue, Wyncote, Philadelphia, frequently make us acknowledge the great distance Pound travelled from his suburban origins in quest of a poetry capable of wrenching the American impulse into art, though, on his own admission, he never succeeded in creating the 'paradiso / terrestre' imagined towards the very end of his carpet-bag of an epic – a work that very few would deny 'soars way above the crowd', as Homer admiringly put it. The father's unwavering pride in his adventurous son is perhaps best captured by a remark Homer made to Louis Zukofsky in the course of the young Objectivist's first visit to Rapallo in 1933. Walking along the beach together one afternoon, Homer pointed out to him a distant figure swimming on his back half a mile from shore: 'See that over there floating? That's my boy!'

London Review of Books (2012)

Review of *Ezra Pound to His Parents: Letters 1895-1929*, edited by Mary de Rachewiltz, A. David Moody, and Joanna Moody (Oxford University Press)

Dark Caverns:
The Correspondence of T.S. Eliot

'It often seems to me very bizarre', T.S. Eliot wrote, at the age of thirty-seven, to his older brother Henry, 'that a person of my antecedents should have had a life like a bad Russian novel'. It's probably Dostoevsky that Eliot had in mind here, about whom he had decidedly mixed feelings. In one of his London Letters for *The Dial*, written shortly before the publication of *The Waste Land* in the autumn of 1922, he observed that the Russian novelist had 'an infinite capacity for taking no pains' with the technical aspects of fiction; on the other hand, he also conceded that Dostoevsky's medical and emotional problems were the catalysts for his genius, suggesting that in his novels 'epilepsy and hysteria cease to be defects of an individual and become – as a fundamental weakness can, given the ability to face it and study it – the entrance to a genuine and personal universe'.

What Eliot seems to be marvelling at in his letter to Henry is the sheer unlikeliness of his journey from his comfortable Unitarian upbringing in St Louis – with summers spent at the family holiday home in East Gloucester – to the extreme state of mind that found expression in *The Waste Land*, with its apocalyptic 'hooded hordes swarming / Over endless plains', its gothic 'bats with baby faces', its horrifying glimpses into atrocity – 'White bodies naked on the low damp ground'; its savage depictions of joyless sex, its unsparing portrayal of intolerable marital relations, its kaleidoscopic refractions of dysfunction and despair. These chunky tomes allow us to follow day by day, drop by harrowing drop, Eliot's 'rudely forced' metamorphosis into the poet of hysteria whose sufferings enabled him, like Dostoevsky, to find 'the entrance to a genuine and personal universe'.

The word 'personal', however, was far from being a term of praise in Eliot's critical vocabulary. He of course wanted his poetry to be 'genuine', or '*echt*', to borrow the term Ezra Pound made use of to separate out the good bits from the bad bits on the drafts of *The Waste Land*; but to be personal was not what Eliot meant, not what he meant at all. Indeed, the ideal of the 'impersonal' lay deep at the core of the aesthetic – and cultural and political – views that he propounded so magisterially in his criticism, and in many of the letters dispatched to his carefully chosen cadre of contributors to the magazine he edited, *The Criterion*, launched in October of 1922, with financial backing from Lady Rothermere. Eliot summed up his concept of the impersonal most famously in his 1919 essay 'Tradition and the Individual Talent'; there he observes that

> the bad poet is usually unconscious where he ought to be conscious, and conscious where he ought to be unconscious. Both errors tend to make him 'personal'. Poetry is not a turning loose of emotion, but an escape from emotion; it is not the expression of personality, but an escape from personality. But, of course, only those who have personality and emotions know what it means to want to escape from these things.

While the whole Tradition versus Individual or Classical versus Romantic debate that this essay played a significant role in kick-starting has now come to seem as spectral as Eliot's unreal commuters flowing over London Bridge, the concept of 'escape' is likely to loom insistently in the thoughts of anyone working their way through these volumes: letter after letter reveals Eliot suffering from overwork, exhaustion, *aboulie* (want of will), emotional derangement, influenza, severe toothache, and impending nervous breakdown. Periodically he reports doctors ordering him to the country, or abroad, to take a complete rest as the only means of staving off some unimaginably dire collapse. Impossibly demanding commitments lour on all sides. 'If there were the sound of water only', one keeps thinking, 'Drip drop drip drop drop drop drop / But there is no water'. Occasionally a howl of despair escapes him: 'In the last ten years', he writes to John Middleton Murry in April of 1925

> gradually, but deliberately – I have made myself into a *machine*. I have done it deliberately – in order to endure, in order not to feel ...

And yet Eliot's multifarious ailments and anxieties pale into insignificance when compared with those of his wife Vivien, whose relentless ill-health and emotional and mental instability provide the dominant motif to swathes of his correspondence. If Eliot, like Dostoevsky, or his own Tiresias in *The Waste Land*, gained entry to his particular rhetorical world through weakness and hysteria, this portal was provided, in no small measure, by the woman whom he married after a courtship of not much more than two months, in June of 1915. The match severely displeased his parents, his father in particular, though it delighted his new friend Ezra Pound. Pound was so eager to keep his prime discovery based in London that he urged the desirability of the union on both parties, and even wrote a long letter, included here, to Eliot's father explaining the ins

and outs of literary London, and the economic prosperity his
protégé would soon be enjoying there.

Eliot aficionados have been kept waiting a long time for
these letters, for reasons that have never been clearly explained.
As his widow Valerie acknowledges in her introduction to
Volume 1 (first issued in 1988, but since expanded with an
extra 200 newly discovered letters), although Eliot was on the
whole inclined not to want his correspondence published, in
his mellow old age he conceded that if Valerie herself would
undertake the task, it wouldn't be in defiance of his wishes. The
over twenty-year delay between the first version of Volume 1
and these subsequent volumes rather encouraged the notion
that a 'smoking gun' lurked somewhere, and that the Estate
was suppressing it. Part of the fascination of Eliot's poetry has
always derived from its ability to suggest that, as in detective
novels, of which he was an avid consumer, somewhere, inside
or outside the poem, there lurked a vital but elusive clue that,
once discovered, would at last reveal all. No such revelation
has emerged, though on occasions Eliot's self-analysis does
deploy terms that send a chill down the spine. The letter
quoted above to Murry continues:

> *but it has killed* V. In leaving the bank I hope to become less a
> machine – but yet I am frightened – because I don't know what
> it will do to me – and to V. – should I come alive again. I have
> deliberately killed my senses – I have deliberately died – in
> order to go on with the outward form of living – This I did in
> 1915. What will happen if I live again? 'I am I' but with what
> feelings, with what results to *others* – Have I the right to be I
> – But the dilemma – to kill another person by being dead, or to
> kill them by being alive? Is it best to make oneself a machine,
> and kill them by not giving nourishment, or to be alive, and

kill them by wanting something that one *cannot* get from that person? Does it happen that two persons' lives are absolutely hostile? Is it true that sometimes one can only live by another's dying?

A footnote alerts us to Sweeney's haunting speech in *Sweeney Agonistes*, the unfinished play with which Eliot was struggling in these years, about the man who once 'did a girl in', and then kept her with 'a gallon of Lysol in a bath'. Like *The Waste Land*, this brilliant fragment was clearly a way for Eliot to model his peculiar marital situation:

> He didn't know if was alive
> > and the girl was dead
> He didn't know if the girl was alive
> > and he was dead
> He didn't know if they were both alive
> > or both were dead

It is striking that Sweeney delivers himself of such thoughts not only to the play's two flighty London flapper-types, Dusty and Doris, but also to a group of visiting Americans, who explain to their hosts that while London is 'a fine place to come on a visit', they couldn't live there: 'London's a little too gay for us / Yes I'll say a little too gay'. One catches in the lines something of Eliot's sense of the unbridgeable gap that had opened up between the reassuring, if 'ungay', America of his family (he embarked on the play a couple of years after a visit from his mother, his sister Marian, and his brother Henry), and the 'bad Russian novel' into which his decision to marry Vivien and attempt to forge a literary career in London had plunged him.

The comprehensive – perhaps, one can occasionally feel, rather *too* comprehensive – policy underlying this edition means we get a full sense of Eliot's antecedents. Volume 1's opening pages are mainly occupied by a string of letters from his mother Charlotte to the Head Master of Milton Academy negotiating entrance for the academic year 1905-06 for the sixteen-year-old Tom, as an alternative to starting immediately at Harvard. Mr Cobb is informed of young Eliot's 'congenital rupture', which required him to wear a truss from an early age, and of her purchase of a 'low steamer trunk' in which she wants his clothes to be kept so that they'll remain free of dust. A request from Tom for permission to swim in a quarry near the Academy elicits a wary demand for more information, since she has seen 'quarry ponds surrounded by steep rock that looked dangerous', while her husband Henry is worried lest Tom catch typhoid. 'One must be so careful these days', as Madame Sosostris would later put it. Eliot Senior's attitude to the changes afoot in society is neatly captured in a letter of 7 March 1914 to his brother, Thomas Lamb Eliot:

> I do not approve of public instruction in Sexual relations. When I teach my children to avoid the Devil I don't begin by giving them a letter of introduction to him and his crowd. I hope that a cure for Syphilis will never be discovered. It is God's punishment for nastiness. Take it away and there will be more nastiness, and it will be necessary to emasculate our children to keep them clean.

It is often suggested that some kind of sexual ambivalence or repression lay at the heart of Eliot's difficulties, and certainly his poetry dramatizes contrasting extremes of male sexuality, swinging from the virginal self-consciousness of J. Alfred

Prufrock to the primitive vigour of Sweeney, or the hero of his long-running smutty epic, the black King Bolo, whose priapic antics were outlined in cringe-making letters to chums such as Wyndham Lewis, Ezra Pound and Bonamy Dobrée. In 1927, in the last of these volumes, we find Eliot committing himself to a forbidding programme of sanctity, chastity, humility, and austerity, yet at around the same period celebrating, in letters to Dobrée, King Bolo's fecund powers in doggerel that would shame a hormonal schoolboy.

The inclusion of numerous letters by Eliot's family and friends, and the extensive footnotes that excerpt liberally from missives received, as well as explicating all references and offering useful mini-biographies of every potential *Criterion* contributor Eliot ever contacted, mean these volumes provide an exhaustively detailed picture of the circumstances in which Eliot's correspondence, and his criticism and his poems, were written. The decision also allows for a range of different perspectives on the Eliots' problems. Having spent a few weeks with Tom and Vivien in Italy in the spring of 1926, Henry furnished his younger brother with a trenchant, no-nonsense diagnosis of Vivien's condition, which he concluded was so much play-acting. Her 'state of emotional anguish is self-induced', he pronounces, 'voluntarily and deliberately. It is something which Vivien herself could put a stop to at any moment, by an effort of will'. Her hallucinations, her threats of suicide, were simply a means to 'secure for herself the notoriety and attention which is meat and drink to her ... The climax of her satisfaction would be to suffer some fate, not extinction, and not too painful, which would be incontestably dramatic'. He urges Eliot either to ignore altogether her 'bag of tricks', or to show her 'that the only impression they make on you is that of utter silliness and puerility'. A bracing view, to which Eliot seems not to have responded, preferring to consign her to the hands of a succession of medical 'experts', the most lethal of whom was a German quack called Dr Karl Bernhard Martin; he prescribed a diet so radically restricted that Vivien ended up suffering severe malnutrition. Henry's unpitying analysis, so at odds with – and perhaps provoked by – Eliot's truly wondrous powers of solicitude in the years covered by these volumes, seems to have reflected the family's general disapproval of Vivien. A letter written by Henry Senior just four days before his death in January of 1919, notes approvingly that his youngest son is doing well in the bank, but curtly adds: 'Wish I liked his wife, but I don't'.

It was a great source of grief to Eliot that his father never lived to see his errant son make good. In his letters home he often works hard to impress with details of his steady upward progress through the echelons of the London literary world, and to pass on the frisson that he clearly felt at rubbing shoulders with well-born literary types in Bloomsbury salons: a typical bulletin to his mother of 22 February, 1920, makes purposeful mention of Lady Ottoline Morrell, Lady Ida Sitwell, Virginia Woolf ('a daughter of Sir Leslie Stephen') and Sydney Waterlow ('Lord Robert Cecil's right hand man').

Eliot's movement away from his antecedents can be traced, then, through these letters, as occurring on a number of different levels. If his hasty marriage ended up leading him deep into the heart of a bad Russian novel, or perhaps a gothic-y English one like *Jane Eyre* (which Eliot taught as a part of his 1918 extension lecture course – he thought it and *Wuthering Heights* 'amazingly good stuff'), it also inaugurated his journey into the mores and conventions of the country whose nationality he would adopt officially in 1927. Virginia Woolf famously described him, in a letter to Clive Bell, as attired in 'a four-piece suit', and these letters show him assuming the language and views of High Toryism with often dismaying completeness. His letters to newspaper editors can make particularly uncomfortable reading. On 8 January 1923 the *Daily Mail* printed a letter he'd written — perhaps partly in the hope of impressing its proprietor, Lord Rothermere, into offering him a job — commending their support of Italian Fascism, as well as the hard line the paper took on Edith Thompson, who was to be hanged the next day for her part in the murder by her lover, Frederick Bywaters, of her husband. 'Nothing could be more salutary', writes Eliot,

> at the present time than the remarkable series of articles which you have been publishing on Fascismo [all, a footnote tells us, highly admiring ones]; these alone constitute a public service of the greatest value and would by themselves have impelled me to write to thank you.

> On the Ilford murder your attitude has been in striking contrast with the flaccid sentimentality of other papers I have seen, which have been so impudent as to affirm that they represented the great majority of the British people.

'Disgusted of Tunbridge Wells', he might have signed himself. Another draws to the public's attention the dangers presented to motorists by charabancs travelling in convoy.

Pound, for one, didn't buy it at all — and began addressing his friend as Old Possum, the implication being that Eliot, having suitably camouflaged himself in the trappings of English society, was simply lying low in the enemy camp. Eliot was willing enough, in his correspondence with Pound, to play along with the notion, and on occasion deployed suitably

Uncle Remus-style lingo in letters and postcards to *il miglior fabbro*. But by 1928, when he defined himself in *For Lancelot Andrews* as 'classicist in literature, royalist in politics, and anglo-catholic in religion', the process of assuming an English identity that we have watched gathering momentum over the previous 14 years might be said to have completed itself. It is of course possible to see Eliot's championing of 'classicism' as a possum-style attempt to obscure the unstable nature of his own inspiration, of the fact, as Randall Jarrell once brilliantly put it, that Eliot was 'one of the most subjective and daemonic poets who ever lived, the victim and helpless beneficiary of his own inexorable compulsions, obsessions'; but his public espousal of royalism and anglo-catholicism can be taken as evidence that he himself felt he had now moved decisively beyond the Unitarian and American democratic traditions in which he'd been raised.

Eliot's principal achievement, it is generally agreed, is his poetry, but one would hardly guess he composed verse at all from a random sampling of these volumes. It wasn't that he was particularly unwilling to discuss 'the intolerable wrestle / With words and meanings' in his letters, but that it seems that months and even years would pass without his attempting to clamber into the ring. In the course of the 870 pages of Volume 3, covering 1926 and 1927, he flickers into life as a poet just once, with the composition of 'Journey of the Magi', which, he tells Conrad Aiken, he wrote 'in three quarters of an hour after church time and before lunch one Sunday morning, with the assistance of half a bottle of Booth's gin'. Manuscript materials may in time reveal that Eliot was pursuing his primary vocation more purposefully than these letters suggest, and it would be particularly interesting to see any drafts relating to *Sweeney Agonistes*, on which he was at work for years, and which he seems to have imagined would be a decisive step beyond *The Waste Land*. In a somewhat surprising move he contacted Arnold Bennett (a novelist much pilloried by modernists such as Woolf and Pound) for advice on writing what Bennett understood would be 'a drama of modern life (furnished flat sort of people) in a rhythmic prose "perhaps with certain things in it accentuated by drum-beats"'. They met a number of times between 1923 and 1925, and Eliot was effusive in his thanks, reporting himself 'tremendously encouraged' by Bennett's advice after one session together in October of 1924, and, as was his wont, rather overdoing the flattery, even insisting Bennett's guidance will make him 'feel that the play will be as much yours as mine'.

After the relative deluge of poems, by Eliot's slow standards, completed in the course of Volume 1, climaxing in the sprawling manuscript of *The Waste Land* and his excited negotiations with Pound over what should be cut from it and what should remain, Eliot's poetic output slowed to a painful trickle. Editors beseeching him for new poems were sternly warned that he not only had nothing to offer them, but was unlikely to produce anything in the foreseeable future. While *The Waste Land*, in its four printings (in *The Criterion* in October 1922, in *The Dial* in November 1922, as a book from Boni and Liveright in New York in December 1922, and as a book from the Woolfs' Hogarth Press in September 1923), was slowly but steadily conquering the literary world, and making Eliot the most respected and influential young poet of the time, he was spending his days working in Lloyds Bank, and devoting every scrap of his free time to editing *The Criterion*.

In the long run his editorship of this magazine led to his appointment as a director of Faber & Gwyer, under whose aegis it was relaunched as *The New Critierion* in January of 1926.

This appointment finally enabled Eliot to resign from Lloyds, and embark on his extremely successful, and financially secure career in publishing. As a gamble, then, it might be said to have paid off, but the years covered by Volume 2 of these letters, 1923–25, present a gruelling account of Eliot burning the candle at both ends, disentangling foreign debt by day, and firing off letters to such as Valéry and Cocteau and Gide (in very serviceable French) and Hugo von Hofmannsthal and Yeats and Gertrude Stein each evening and at weekends. For those, such as Pound, who believed a poet as gifted as Eliot should spend as much of his time as possible writing poetry, the assumption of the enormous workload involved in running a respectable quarterly more or less single-handed, though with some help from Vivien, when she was well enough, and a part-time secretary, was simply baffling – and Pound didn't think much of the results of Eliot's labours either, characterizing *The Criterion*'s contributors as a 'bunch of dead mushrooms'. Its circulation never rose much above 800, it always ran at a loss, Eliot received no salary for editing it, and it consumed inordinate amounts of his time.

It had, though, a polemical purpose. Though he liked to present the magazine as serenely above party politics, his overall hope was, as he put it to a prospective contributor, 'to give to Toryism the intellectual basis with the illusion of which Socialism has so long deceived the young and eager'. His idea was to gather around him a band of the like-minded, with principles debated and agreed upon at monthly *Criterion* dinners; and while not exactly disciples, such as Herbert Read and Richard Aldington and Bonamy Dobrée were to an extent marshalled by Eliot into a phalanx that could be roughly relied upon to deliver *Criterion* doctrine; although when Aldington – who in later years would break decisively with Eliot –

submitted a long, over-enthusiastic essay on D. H. Lawrence, it was rejected on the grounds that it failed to 'fall in with the general position of the *Criterion*', a formulation frequently used in letters returning material that Eliot didn't want to print. But perhaps what is most striking about the magazine, in these early years, is the exemplary thoroughness with which Eliot sought out contributions from a really extensive range of European writers, and attempted to cover intellectual developments not only in France, Germany, Italy, and Spain, but Holland, Russia, and Denmark – and even America.

Still, even the keenest fans of Eliot are going to find the great mass of *Criterion* business correspondence assembled in Volumes 2 and 3 of these letters hard going. Many were dictated to his secretary, and although crisply phrased, are essentially of no interest – and made me wonder about the 'minor letters' excluded from Volume 3 to keep the book to 'a relatively manageable length'. And despite Eliot's prestigious roll-call of contributors, and his own brilliance as a review-essayist, *The Criterion* itself, while always high-minded, is not always that riveting. Its sponsor, Lady Rothermere, who had hoped for something a little more social and glitzy, frequently and frankly complained that it was boring, to which Eliot could do nothing but agree and apologize. And what imp of the perverse made him open the first issue with an essay by George Saintsbury on 'Dullness'?

The magazine did, however, play a considerable role in Eliot's emergence as the most authoritative literary and, to some, cultural spokesman of the day. When, much to Eliot's credit, he accepted Hart Crane's 'The Tunnel' (which would become part VII of *The Bridge*) for publication, Crane excitedly fired off a letter to his patron, Otto Kahn, in which he described Eliot as 'representative of the most exacting literary standards of our times', and this acceptance proof that Kahn was backing a winner. By 1927 Eliot is not quite yet the Pope of Russell Square, but he's well on the way to becoming him. Eliot's success in reconfiguring notions of what constituted successful or valuable poetry can hardly be overestimated. His technical innovations were imitated by many of his verse-writing correspondents (slavishly by such as Conrad Aiken and Archibald MacLeish, creatively by such as Crane, and Allen Tate, and of course Pound); more crucial for the success of the literary revolution that he fomented, however, was his presentation in his critical essays of his own work as the inevitable next step in the history of poetry.

Three years before publishing *The Waste Land* Eliot had already described, in 'Tradition and the Individual Talent', the way a 'new work of art' would alter 'the *whole* existing order' of all previous works of art – which is exactly what happened in the years after 1922. In the extraordinary reviews and essays he wrote between 1916 – when he received his first commission, courtesy of an introduction by Bertrand Russell, for a piece in the *International Journal of Ethics* – and, say, his essay on Milton of 1936, Eliot transformed the genre of literary criticism more dramatically than any writer before him, or since. The charisma, the intelligence, the sophistication, the erudition, the feline but utterly compelling sensibility on display in these essays can make them at times seem like an elaborate literary seduction. Of course the vision of the canon they propound is a highly individual one: Milton bad, Donne good, Shelley very, very bad, Dante very, very good … But Eliot's rhetorical genius was such that his judgements came to seem to many not just a reflection of his own subjective tastes, but infallible verdicts, final and true: in other words 'impersonal'.

Eliot's assumption of the role of quasi-divine gatekeeper of the literary pantheon grows steadily more authoritative as these letters progress. With it comes a weariness that can at times register almost as post-traumatic calm; even when only in his late thirties Eliot speaks repeatedly not just of 'growing older', as he puts it in a letter of 22 August 1927 to his brother, but of having grown definitively 'Old'. Like 'impersonal', 'mature' is one of Eliot's most fulsome terms of approbation, and the Eliot of, say, 'Ash Wednesday' (1930), on which he would soon embark, figures himself maturely and serenely above the fray, an 'agèd eagle' stretching his wings. But his friend and colleague Geoffrey Faber — the deus ex machina, one might say, who finally freed Eliot from his fetters to the bank — was worried by these ascetic tendencies; he felt that a certain element of the dogmatic was creeping into Eliot's life, and imperilling him. In a brave and searching letter of 15 September 1927 Faber ventured some thoughtful criticisms:

> It is not right that you should chain yourself to a routine — it will cramp your mind, & ultimately be fatal to you both as poet & critic, if for no other reason than that it will divorce you further & further from the common man. I cannot help at times suspecting that the difficulties are, to some extent, of your own forging.

Earlier in the letter Faber complains of the 'excessive obscurity' of Eliot's poetry — somewhat ironically given the contribution this excessively obscure work would eventually play in the financial success of his publishing venture — and asks, 'Is it an unavoidable element in your poetry? or is it deliberate?'

The *bon vivant* Faber's bluff, well-meaning, but also acutely probing questions ask us to ponder both the difficulty of

Eliot's poetry, and the difficulties of his life. How 'unavoidable' was it that a poet who had written, in 1915, a prose poem called 'Hysteria' about a man who imagines himself being swallowed by a woman with whom he is having tea, to the point that he is 'lost finally in the dark caverns of her throat, bruised by the ripple of unseen muscles', should that year marry a woman who would induct him into 'dark caverns' from which, as his letter to Murry put it, the only escape, it could at times seem, was to kill her or kill himself? A secure and un-difficult life as a Professor of Philosophy at Harvard was open to Eliot as late as 1919; it held, however, no appeal for him, as he makes clear in a letter to his old Philosophy tutor, J.H. Woods, who had offered him a position in the department. In declining Eliot figures himself somewhat in the image of a Jamesian expatriate, like Lambert Strether of *The Ambassadors*, one who has grown addicted to the complexities of European society, however excruciating the pain they inflict, and would find life back in America insufferably dull. 'I have acquired', he informs Woods, 'the habit of a society so different that it is difficult to find common terms to define the difference'. Something in Eliot, in other words, sought difficulty, wanted, whatever the cost, blood shaking his heart, to raise the stakes, to exchange the unthreatening blandness of Unitarianism, and American culture at large, as he saw it, for something more complex and extreme: a vision, after much purgatorial suffering, of redemption in Heaven; or of fear, in a handful of dust, of damnation in Hell.

New York Review of Books (2012)

Review of *The Letters of T.S. Eliot: Volume 1 (1888-1922)* edited by Valerie Eliot and Hugh Haughton, *The Letters of T.S. Eliot: Volume 2 (1923-1925)* edited by Valerie Eliot and Hugh Haughton, and *The Letters of T.S. Eliot: Volume 3 (1926-1927)* edited by Valerie Eliot and John Haffenden (Yale University Press)

Who Seeketh Thy Woob?
Samuel Greenberg and Hart Crane

In late 1925 Hart Crane set about compiling some notes intended to help Eugene O'Neill write a foreword to Crane's first volume, *White Buildings*, which was to be published by Boni and Liveright the following year. This proved in the end a challenge to which the playwright, even with Crane's guidance, was unable to rise, and Allen Tate had to be called upon to introduce the bard from Akron to the world. Crane's explication of his poetic ideals and practices, however, survived, and was posthumously published in 1937. 'It is as though', he wrote in it, 'a poem gave the reader as he left it a single, new *word*, never before spoken and impossible to actually enunciate, but self-evident as an active principle in the reader's consciousness henceforward'.

Just under two years earlier Crane had come across the work of an unpublished poet with a similar penchant for words 'never before spoken', words such as pussel, orbly, dite, stally, irragulate, swedge, gentlety, and woob. 'This poet, Greenberg', enthused Crane in a letter to his friend Gorham Munson, 'was a Rimbaud in embryo. Did you ever see some of the hobbling yet really gorgeous attempts that boy made without any education or time except when he became confined to a cot? ... No grammar, nor spelling, and scarcely any form, but a quality that is unspeakably eerie and the most convincing gusto. One little poem is as good as any of the consciously-conceived "Pierrots" of Laforgue'. Crane was so impressed that he typed up some 41 poems from Greenberg's chaotic handwritten manuscripts, and then fashioned a poem, 'Emblems of Conduct', composed almost entirely of lines borrowed from this 'Rimbaud in embryo'.

The strange case of Samuel Greenberg and Hart Crane came to light only by chance. In 1936, Crane's first biographer, Philip Horton, received a package from Mrs T.W. Simpson, the caretaker of the plantation on the Isle of Pines, just off Cuba, that was owned by Crane's mother's family. Crane had spent the summer of 1926 there, working on *The Bridge*, but had had to pack up and leave in haste when a hurricane struck the island in late October. Four years after Crane's death in 1932, Mrs Simpson dispatched to Horton a package containing a manuscript of 'nineteen sheets of cheap yellow foolscap covered with typewritten poems', no doubt assuming that they were by Crane. A little detective work revealed that they weren't, though several of them, ('Conduct', 'The Laureate', 'Perusal', 'Immortality', and 'Daylight') at once struck Horton as familiar, for they had been cannibalized for 'Emblems of Conduct', while various phrases from Greenberg such as 'vanished lily grove' and 'crested herb', appear in drafts of 'Voyages', the sonnet sequence with which *White Buildings* concludes.[1]

It is, I think, safe to say that without Crane's feverish, if temporary interest in the work of Greenberg, only the handful of poems that his friend William Murrell Fisher managed to get printed in the Woodstock magazine *The Plowshare* would ever have seen the light of day. However uncomfortable we may feel about Crane's plagiarizing of lines from Greenberg's work to create a poem of his own, this act

[1] This was first pointed out by Marc Simon in his thorough and judicious study *Samuel Greenberg, Hart Crane and the Lost Manuscripts* (Humanities Press: Atlantic Highlands, NJ, 1978), to which I am much indebted.

of theft did indubitably end up preserving Greenberg's name and work from oblivion.[2] The whole affair also, however, reveals much about the possibilities and pressures shaping Crane's early development, and the lineaments of his uneasy, conflicted search for a niche in the modernist pantheon as it evolved in the 1920s.

The primal scene occurred in Woodstock in December of 1923. Crane was staying with his friend Slater Brown and the painter Edward Nagle. On a number of occasions they visited the English-born William Murrell Fisher. Fisher, it seems, never felt quite at ease with the exuberant poet; finding himself alone with Crane one day, he cast about for something that might interest him. He had in his possession five of Samuel Greenberg's poetic notebooks, and offered to show them. Although Crane, as Fisher later recalled, 'opened the package very dubiously, when his eye lighted on some of the poems, he became very excited. He flared up in a corner with it'. Crane asked to borrow the notebooks for a few days, a few days that turned into several weeks; the loan resulted in the nineteen pages of Greenberg's work that Crane transcribed, and only abandoned nearly three years later on the Isle of Pines, as well, of course, as 'Emblems of Conduct'.

The sad story of Samuel Greenberg's life was certainly one likely to appeal to Crane's notion of the poet as romantic victim. He was born in Vienna in 1893, the sixth of eight children. In 1900 his family joined the mass emigration of Jews from Europe to America, settling on the Lower East Side. Greenberg's father, Jacob, earned a living embroidering

---

[2] In his Preface to the 1947 edition of Greenberg's poems edited by Harold Holden and Jack McManis, Allen Tate revealed that Crane wanted to drop 'Emblems of Conduct' from *White Buildings*, but was talked into including it by Malcolm Cowley and Tate himself. Tate also declares Crane's '"plagiarism"' to be, in his opinion, 'quite legitimate'.

silver and gold brocade for ark of Torah scrolls, but on occasions the family clearly lived close to the bread line. In an autobiographical text Greenberg talks of his 'sleepy-cave of rats and cabbage, sawdust floor'. He had to leave school at 14 to help out in his father's workshop, and that same year, 1908, his mother died, possibly of tuberculosis, a disease he contracted himself about four years later. It was while recuperating in various hospitals that he began filling notebooks and almost any other bits of paper that he came across with hundreds and hundreds of poems and drafts of verse plays. 'This boy', wrote James Laughlin in his introduction to a selection of Greenberg's work published by New Directions in 1939, 'was drunk on words and he poured them forth with a wild, chaotic passion – producing, occasionally, lines of startling beauty and power'. Greenberg died in 1917 in Sea View Hospital on Staten Island, a few months short of his 24th birthday.

Like so many of his neighbors on the Lower East Side, Greenberg grew up speaking German, Yiddish, and then English. He never, as he acknowledged, quite mastered 'grammatic truth' in the last of these, as almost any poem of his will illustrate: 'Ah! thus fathomed crowns earnestly will woe thee!' ('Sorrows'); 'Hast thou beaten beauty's cleaves / That tend unwont to spiritual griefs?' ('Appreciation'); 'The perfect gauze can irragulate prophecy / 'Pon serious tempo, blame serene ratio / As string-adhered charm does to love!' ('Odds and Ends'). His prose is often similarly wonky – consider this moving description of his mother's death:

> Life was now a spongy condition. Our mother gradually
> became ill: ear trouble, germ trouble, nose trouble, skull trouble
> – death trouble resulted and the family buried her somewhere
> on Long Island, where a cemetery called Washington was the
> grave for many poor victims, as our unpraised love was settled.

We returned to a café near the doom place, where gathered a
party of thirty or more, ate cheese and eggs with a schooner of
beer and coffee. The rituals of the Jewish religion demand that
one remain seated for seven days upon the floor. Well, we sat on
soft cushions (the angels of wealth!). Thus ended a sorrowful,
meaningless jubilee in an empty, beautiful world, with scarce a
flower knowing joy.

According to his older brother Morris, Sam, as he was known,
was often to be found with his nose in a thesaurus or dictionary,
and in both his poetry and prose one finds him happily
savouring the sounds of words without, one feels, being too
bothered about their precise meaning: 'O burning statue of
tendons!' he expostulates in a lyric entitled 'Man', creating an
image worthy of Raymond Roussel; 'O perfect lay of deity's
crested herb' rhapsodically opens one of his many Sonnets of
Apology also called 'Man'. What exactly, one wonders, did
he mean to convey through the most striking of his nonce
words, 'woob'?[3] Here are some of the various ways in which
he uses it:

Uplift the sordid earth from dark slumber
And deviate spirits' mystic woob ...

('The Laureate')

O birth, O blossom
Has unveiled slumbered woob, there divine, but guarded nigh.

('Religion')

[3] In Greenberg's manuscripts the B is always capitalized, i.e. 'wooB'. The textual issues
raised by Greenberg's originals somewhat resemble those that bedevil editors of a poet

as in saintly
Passions unfelt to lay before
Humbly, a quest: who seeketh thy woob?

('Home')

But shadows, rays from the woob of
All power darkening concept, unfold
The density of birth's hold ...

('Greatness')

such as John Clare. To what extent should Greenberg's non-standard spelling and syntax be amended? In his short 1939 selection for his own New Directions, James Laughlin kept fairly close to Greenberg's originals, but Harold Holden and Jack McManis decided, for their trade edition of 1947 that was published by Henry Holt, to correct his unorthodox spellings of even fairly common words ('ralitives', 'religeon', 'auther', 'enfluence'), and his erratic capitalizations. They also added punctuation. Had Greenberg submitted and had accepted a manuscript for publication in his lifetime, his editor would undoubtedly have insisted the texts be regularized somewhat in the manner of Holden and McManis's edition. In their introduction they observe:

> The problems of editing Greenberg are numerous. Illiterate spelling, 'original' syntax or none at all, archaisms and words of his own invention – these and the illegibility of the pencil script in which much of the poetry is written made the difficulties seem at times insurmountable.

In 2000 Michael Smith launched a superb website http://logopoeia.com/greenberg that presents a sizeable percentage of Greenberg's work in versions that adhere closely to the manuscripts, and in 2005 edited, with Michael Carr, an original spelling edition (*Self Charm: Selected Sonnets & Other Poems* (Katalanché Press)). My quotations in this essay are mainly drawn from the cleaned-up versions offered by McManis and Holden, on the grounds that had Greenberg seen a volume of his work go into print, his numerous elementary spelling errors would undoubtedly have been corrected. I have, however, used the versions transcribed by Crane himself, which are published in an appendix to Simon's study of Greenberg and Crane, for the poems that he cannibalized for 'Emblems of Conduct'. I include in a footnote as well the original Greenberg version of Crane's main source, 'Conduct', and strongly advise anyone interested in Greenberg in his raw state to visit Smith's website.

And still the cast of yearly unnumbered woob
My love did plead at the summer spray.

('Words')

That of quaintly sieving grain doth hint
Extricable details of charms that they
Contain, or of characterism's woob
Of tempo ...

('Sun, Moon, Stars')

Thou who in thy woob has promising content,
Leaves traces of soul's amendments
Enduring infallible discipline ...

('Desires')

Could it be a combination of womb and web, wonder Harold
Holden and Jack McManis in their introduction to their
1947 edition of Greenberg's poems. We will probably never
know, but undoubtedly such freedom from anxiety about
the accepted conventional meanings of words was of great
appeal to Crane, who, in a letter of 1926 to Harriet Monroe,
the editor of *Poetry*, strongly argued for the poet's right to use
words in a manner beyond what he calls their 'logically rigid
significations':

> To put it more plainly, as a poet I may very possibly be
> more interested in the so-called illogical impingements of
> the connotations of words on the consciousness (and their
> combinations and interplay in metaphor on this basis) than

> I am interested in the preservation of their logically rigid
> significations at the cost of limiting my subject matter and
> perceptions involved in the poem.

Crane is here preparing the ground for a defence of his highly
elliptical 'At Melville's Tomb'. Although no surrealist, Crane
claims the right of a poet to 'another logic', one which creates
meanings 'quite independent of the original definition of
the word or phrase or image thus employed'. In answer to
Monroe's query as to how *dice* can *bequeath* an *embassy* in lines 2
and 3 of the first stanza ('The dice of drowned men's bones he
saw bequeath / An embassy') he explains:

> Dice bequeath an embassy, in the first place, by being ground
> (in this connection only, of course) in little cubes from the
> bones of drowned men by the action of the sea, and are finally
> thrown up on the sand, having 'numbers' but no identification.
> These being the bones of dead men who never completed
> their voyage, it seems legitimate to refer to them as the only
> surviving evidence of certain messages undelivered, mute
> evidence of certain things, experiences that the dead mariners
> might have had to deliver. Dice as a symbol of chance and
> circumstance is also employed.

Crane's formidably compressed and initially baffling lines
can, then, with a little help from the author, be parsed into
meaning, but even when they've been decoded they retain an
irreducible strangeness. They certainly fail Pound's test that a
poem should strike the reader as something that could actually
be said in real life. This, to use Crane's term about Greenberg,
is what makes them 'eerie', off-kilter, perplexing; perhaps the
only context in which one can imagine coming across them

in real life is in the homework of a foreign language student working to improve his or her English, and making copious use of dictionary and thesaurus.

One of the reasons Greenberg's non-standard English made Crane 'flare up' was because it modelled a naïve and exhilarating freedom from irony and clarity of the kind that Eliot and Pound were making central to modernist poetics. John T. Irwin suggests in his recent *Hart Crane's Poetry: Appollinaire Lived in Paris, I Live in Cleveland, Ohio* that T.S. Eliot was 'the most important twentieth-century influence on Crane', and certainly *The Bridge* is unimaginable without *The Waste Land*. But Crane also wanted his poetry to develop in ways quite antithetical to Eliot's, as he explained in a letter of 12 June, 1922 to Allen Tate:

> In his own realm Eliot presents us with an absolute *impasse*, yet
> oddly enough, he can be utilized to lead us to, intelligently
> point to, other positions and 'pastures new'. Having absorbed
> him enough we can trust ourselves as never before, in the air
> or on the sea. I, for instance, would like to leave a few of his
> 'negations' behind me, risk the realm of the obvious more, in
> quest of new sensations, *humeurs*.

It is surely telling that the poet with whom Crane favorably contrasts Greenberg in the letter he wrote to Munson from Woodstock in December of 1923 is the poet Eliot had always accredited with most helping him find his voice, Jules Laforgue. But while Laforgue led Eliot towards the 'consciously-created' ironies of 'The Love Song of J. Alfred Prufrock', Greenberg, or so Crane seems to hope, will lead him in the opposite direction, towards 'other positions and "pastures new"' – although not exactly, at least in a poem such as 'At Melville's

Tomb', towards 'the realm of the obvious'. In a further twist, however, Crane's reference to Laforgue in his letter suggests that the relationship that he anticipates evolving between himself and the work of Greenberg will be analogous to the highly creative one that evolved between Eliot and the work of Laforgue; in other words, Crane seems to be buying into an Eliotic model of a poet needing, to develop, a relationship with a dead minor precursor, but choosing a poet as different as possible from the sophisticated, world-weary Laforgue who acted as a catalyst for Eliot.

A letter to Munson written on 26 November, 1921, just over two years before his discovery of Greenberg, indicates the degree of deliberation with which Crane set about searching for the right precursor. 'I don't want to imitate Eliot of course, – but I have come to the stage now where I want to carefully choose my most congenial influences and, in a way, "cultivate" their influence'. In the same letter he mentions having read Eliot's 'Sacred Grove' – as if one defence against being influenced by Eliot were to get the titles of his books wrong. In *The Sacred Wood* he would of course have come across another of Eliot's disquisitions on the relationship between a poet and other poets in the essay on Philip Massinger: 'Immature poets imitate; mature poets steal; bad poets deface what they take, and good poets make it into something better, or at least something different. The good poet welds his theft into a whole of feeling which is unique, utterly different from that from which it was torn; the bad poet throws it into something which has no cohesion'. In a further irony, then, in stealing from a precursor poet who, it was hoped, would allow him to escape the influence of Eliot, he was putting into practice Eliot's own theory of poetic theft, and the acts of appropriation he took it to license. 'There are parts of his

"Gerontion"', Crane marvels in the same letter to Munson, 'that you can find almost bodily in Webster and Johnson [i.e. Ben Jonson]'. In assembling 'Emblems of Conduct' from various Greenberg poems, Crane was, to use a golfing phrase, going to school on Eliot's putt.

And perhaps the most succinct way of describing what Crane does to the lines from 'Conduct' and various other Greenberg poems which he borrowed, or stole, to make his own poem, is to say that he translates them into the Eliotic: Crane, it seems to me, subjects Greenberg to exactly those Eliotic pressures of irony and disillusionment that he hoped, and anticipated, absorption in Greenberg's work would enable him to escape. For the poem makes best sense when considered within an Eliotic framework as a lament for lost wholeness and spiritual revelation, and a condemnation of the trivializing culture of modernity.

> By a peninsula the wanderer sat and sketched
> The uneven valley graves. While the apostle gave
> Alms to the meek the volcano burst
> With sulphur and aureate rocks ...
> For joy rides in stupendous coverings
> Luring the living into spiritual gates.
>
> Orators follow the universe
> And radio the complete laws to the people.
> The apostle conveys thought through discipline.
> Bowls and cups fill historians with adorations, –
> Dull lips commemorating spiritual gates.
>
> The wanderer later chose this spot of rest
> Where marble clouds support the sea

And where was finally borne a hero.
By that time summer and smoke were past.
Dolphins still played, arching the horizons,
But only to build memories of spiritual gates.

In a fine interpretation in his *Poetry of Hart Crane* (1968), R.W.B. Lewis demonstrated how the poem can be read as a meditation on belatedness and the dilemmas of modernity. The 'wanderer' of the first line is an artist figure, one with an obvious interest in ultimate meanings, which is why he is sketching 'graves'. The religious implications of the term 'apostle' suggest that he too is concerned with the spiritual, devoting his time to practical charity, giving 'alms to the meek'. Meanwhile, a volcano bursts 'with sulphur and aureate rocks'. This eruption evokes the 'mighty fountain' 'momently forced' in Coleridge's 'Kubla Khan', 'Amid whose swift half-intermitted burst / Huge fragments vaulted like rebounding hail / Or chaffy grain beneath the thresher's flail'. Both Coleridge's and Crane's eruptions fuse the revolutionary, the spiritual, the natural, and the (male) sexual. In 'Kubla Khan' the eruption 'flings up momently the sacred river', and in 'Emblems of Conduct' we learn that this outburst of joy or mystical eruption lures 'the living into spiritual gates'; this may seem a somewhat paradoxical idea, since gates suggest enclosure, whereas 'spiritual' implies some transcendent realm beyond all enclosures, but Kubla Khan's response to the eruption is also to enclose the sacred river it throws up ('So twice five miles of fertile ground / With walls and towers were girdled round'). Thus the wanderer might be compared with Coleridge in his post-visionary state seeking to recover his dangerous primal revelation, or, to borrow an analogy from another famous romantic poem, Keats's knight in 'La

Belle Dame Sans Merci' awaking on the cold hillside in a state of post-coital disenchantment, condemned to sketch uneven valley graves.

One of the most influential ways by which Eliot 'modernized himself', as Pound put it, was by demonstrating the impossibility of such romantic self-figurations for the early twentieth-century poet. In accordance with this Eliotic perspective on modernity, Crane's second stanza sets about dramatizing the way the ideal of the spiritual is ruthlessly exploited or perverted in the contemporary world. Like Eliot, Crane attacks popular rational, scientific or political interpretations of existence, such as those delivered by the orators who 'radio the complete laws to the people'. The apostle's thought, on the other hand, conveyed through discipline, registers as at once remote from contemporary concerns, and as dispiritingly joyless. The historians complete the diagnosis: their dry, solemn 'adorations' of ancient bowls and cups are a far cry from the 'stupendous' joy experienced by the Magi when adoring the infant Christ, the story of whose birth is the supreme example of a revolutionary eruption that changed the world.

In the final stanza Crane surveys the aftermath of a revelatory experience, showing how literary history, or civilization generally, neutralizes the visionary moment, even if it results in a lasting work of art. Its images are insistently elegiac. The 'marble clouds' supporting the sea in the wanderer's 'spot of rest' suggest some vast mausoleum. He may turn out to be a 'chosen hero', that is a saint or canonized poet, but the poem's point is to demonstrate the unbridgeable distance between the overwhelming spiritual revelation of the volcano and the belated present: 'By that time summer and smoke were past' – the phrase 'summer and smoke', incidentally, was in turn lifted by Tennessee Williams for his 1948 play of that title. The dolphins leaping out of the sea, only to return to it, are presented as symbolic of the repeated failure of modern attempts at transcendence; their 'arching' serves merely to 'build memories of spiritual gates', that is to remind us of what we can no longer reach.

Here is the Greenberg material that Crane transformed:

Conduct

By a peninsula, the painter sat and
sketched the uneven valley graves
The apostle gave alms to the
Meek, the volcano burst
In fusive sulphor and hurled
Rocks and ore into the air,
Heaven's sudden change at
The drawing tempestuous
Darkening shade of dense clouded hues
The wanderer soon chose
His spot of rest, they bore the
Chosen hero upon their shoulders
Whom they strangely admired – as
The Beach tide summer of people desired.[4]

---

[4] By a peninsula, the painter sat and
Sketched the uneven vally groves
The apostle gave alms to the
Meek, the valcano burst
In fusive sulphor and hurled
Rocks and ore into the air
Heaven's sudden change at
The drawing tempestious
Darkening shade of Dense clouded Hues

Crane's 'For joy rides in stupendous coverings', is adapted from line 13 of 'The Laureate', which runs 'For joy hides its stupendous coverings', and his refrain, the repeated line ending 'spiritual gates', is taken from 'Immortality', which both opens and closes with these four lines, though the punctuation varies somewhat:

> But only to be memories of spiritual gates
> Letting us feel the difference from the real
> Are not limits the sooth to formulate
> Theories thereof, simply our ruler to feel?

The lines about the orator and the apostle in stanza two derive from 'Perusal', lines 8-12:

> The apostle
> Reigns over the community in conveying
> His thoughtful discipline through
> Speech. The orator follows the universe
> And refrains the laws of the people ...

The historians' bowls and cups are adapted from lines 8-10 of 'Immortality':

> The museums of the ancient, fine stones
> For bowls and cups, found historians
> Sacred adorations, the numismatist hath shown
> But only to be memories of spiritual gates ...

> The wanderer soon chose
> His spot of rest, they bore the
> Chosen hero upon their shoulders
> Whom they strangely admired – as,
> The Beach tide Summer of people desired.

Note in particular Crane's transcription of 'groves' as 'graves'.

Finally, line 11 of 'Daylight' features 'floating marble like clouds'.

The most striking aspect of the appropriation is the way that Crane, in the words of the critic L.S. Dembo, 'changed the whole tone of Greenberg's work from romantic enthusiasm to irony'. Yet, as in the line and a half from 'At Melville's Tomb' that Crane explicated to Monroe, strangeness persists, even after it becomes clear that the poem can be made to fit the Eliot-inspired New Critical model of the mordant, ironic, modernist lyric. In this case the strangeness comes from Greenberg, whose language is so at odds with the Eliotic template imposed on it by Crane; but it is precisely in this 'at oddness' that we approach both the pathos of Crane's dilemma –a pathos that seems to me to lie at the heart of the expressiveness of his contorted poetic idiom – and his authentic originality, contradictory though it may seem to talk of originality in relation to a poem plagiarized from Greenberg according to Eliotic principles and then made to embody an Eliotic vision. Crane wanted, *needed* this strangeness or 'eeriness', to use his own term, for it functions as his strongest form of resistance to the pressures of Eliotic modernism; it boldly delivers his sense of the marginalization that he shared with Greenberg, and it effectively registers his defiant difference from both Eliot and from Eliot's admirers and imitators, such as Allen Tate and John Crowe Ransom. In other words, the drive to be assimilated into the modernist canon, and the drive *not* to be assimilated into it, were almost equally strong in Crane. Greenberg spoke eloquently to him of all that is antithetical to the modernist vision of a disillusioned band of the elect sifting through the ruins of civilization, of all that retains its distinctiveness and weirdness in defiance of the 'orators' who 'radio the complete laws to the people', and the apostles who convey 'thought through discipline'. Indeed, with hindsight it can be difficult not to glimpse an image of the future Pope of Russell Square and his earnest disciples in the first three lines of the second stanza of 'Emblems of Conduct', and even of Crane's own death by water in the wanderer's choice of his spot of rest near the arching dolphins at the poem's close.

Crane's acute sense of his own belatedness results then, in this collaged poem, in the severe disciplining of the spontaneity and impulsiveness that Crane initially found so exciting when he was introduced by Fisher to Greenberg's notebooks. At the same time, its occluded source in a poet whose English was erratic but whose work communicated a most unEliotic 'gusto' pulls it in the opposite direction. 'Emblems of Conduct' could also be said to act out in miniature Crane's ongoing disagreements with such as Tate and Yvor Winters over the kind of relationship Eliotic modernism might develop with the American tradition that Eliot so firmly rejected; Whitman was the focus of these arguments, and by aligning himself in the 'Cape Hatteras' section of *The Bridge* with the great grey poet ('My hand / in yours, / Walt Whitman − / so − ') Crane was effectively flinging down a gauntlet, one which Winters picked up by declaring in a brutal review that the poem merely illustrated 'the impossibility of getting anywhere with the Whitmanian inspiration'. It was Emerson, rather than Whitman, who provided the stimulus to Greenberg's poetic rhapsodies, as evidenced most obviously by his highly Emersonian titles such as 'Philosophy', 'Reflection', 'Necessity', 'Existence' and so on. Fisher records giving Greenberg a copy of Emerson's *Essays* soon after they first met in New York in 1912, feeling the young poet was working in something of a vacuum: when Fisher asked him in the course of this meeting what Greenberg had been reading, he was astonished to receive the reply, 'The Dictionary'.

Emerson clearly brought Greenberg to the boil, as he had done Whitman some 60 years earlier. Greenberg's numerous 'Sonnets of Apology' show the influence most clearly, channeling much transcendentalist uplift and instruction in their conjugations of various general topics, but in the process subjecting the Emersonian to baffling, almost cyclonic forces of distortion and disruption. Here are some openings:

> O science of fibrous crested lyre,
> Who, winding, heeds our inmost desire,
> Can heave a spirit from now and then,
> Thus cleave the depth from perspiring spleen ...

('The Etude')

> Gluttonous helium of thought's endowment,
> What piercing awe hast thou bestowed!

('Memory')

> Whose wean left thee empty, O 'pelling guise,
> Where in thy power's depth doth crave
> Inevitable season, that of Holy Spirit sustained,
> Why must I knight my future grave?

('Necessity')

Greenberg's 'gusto' comes from the way his poetry reveals him in the act of intrepidly adventuring into both a foreign language and a new ideology, and the peculiarity of his idiom is movingly expressive of the immigrant condition, in both its excitement and its awkwardness. The hyperbolic rapturousness is particularly striking given the desperate circumstances in which Greenberg composed his poems, whose dominant feeling one might gloss as 'in for a penny, in for a pound'. His 17 notebooks, which are now in the Fales Collection of the New York University Library, present, among other things, a touching record of the desires and difficulties inherent in the first-generation immigrant experience of assimilation.

Crane is not the only poet to have thought it worth seeking out Greenberg's woob. 'If you haven't read the poems I recommend them highly', wrote Elizabeth Bishop to Robert Lowell in a letter of 1950. 'He was certainly one of the finest poetic *characters* I know anything about, and [his] phrases are magnificent – and no critic has ever apparently appreciated either at their real value'. I first came across his name in Frank O'Hara's 1960 poem 'Cornkind' where his life is improbably imagined as inspiring a film starring Bette Davis:

> what of Bette Davis in
> AN EVENING WITH WILLIAM MORRIS
> or THE WORLD OF SAMUEL GREENBERG

> what of Hart Crane
> what of phonograph records and gin

O'Hara's fellow New York School poet John Ashbery included in his 2007 collection *A Worldly Country* a poem entitled 'Of the "East" River's Charm' (an allusion to Greenberg's 'East River's Charm'); the poem, a subheading tells us, was written in 'homage to Samuel Greenberg', and it includes as epigraph two lines from Greenberg's 'Ballad on Joy'. Bishop, O'Hara and Ashbery might all, like Crane, be said to explore adversarial stances towards many of the assumptions encoded in Eliot's brand of modernism, and in particular to its ideal of the centripetal – 'the still point of the turning world'. The highly centrifugal WORLD OF SAMUEL GREENBERG is more like an ongoing stream of language, an 'unassigned frequency' to borrow an image from Ashbery's 'Self-Portrait in a Convex Mirror', that one can tune in to pretty much at random. His work reminds us that both the naïve or primitive and the postmodern share the notion that poetry or art can happen any time, any place, a point perhaps gestured to in 'Of the "East" River's Charm':

> Manna fell to the ground in streamers
> and this was OK,
> I heard someone say.

Along with Walt Whitman and William Carlos Williams, Crane was one of the poets that O'Hara singled out in the spoof manifesto 'Personism' as 'better than the movies'. Greenberg undoubtedly played some part in helping Crane to write the poetry that meant so much to O'Hara. For, in his restless and often frustrating quest for a means of moving beyond the *impasse* with which Eliot's poetry presented him, Crane found in the five notebooks of Greenberg's showed to him by Fisher in Woodstock in December of 1923, a tantalizing glimpse of a viable poetic future, as well as a compelling distraction from phonograph records and gin.

New Walk (2013)

Industrious Auden

In August of 1955, in the middle of his annual summer sojourn on the Italian island of Ischia, W.H. Auden received from Dr Enid Starkie, the distinguished author of books on Baudelaire and Rimbaud and a lecturer in Modern Languages at the University of Oxford, a letter inviting him to stand as a candidate for the Oxford Professorship of Poetry. This five-year post was about to be vacated by Cecil Day-Lewis, the back legs of that mythical beast McSpaunday (MacNeice, Spender, Auden, Day-Lewis) which had rampaged through British poetical and political circles of the 1930s, warning the old gang that their time was up, threatening mayhem, revolution, bloodshed: 'Don't bluster, Bimbo', Day-Lewis had, not entirely convincingly, threatened, 'it won't do you any good; / We can be much ruder and we're learning to shoot'.

It was Auden's evasion of the task of shooting at, or at least playing a role in the fight against, Nazi Germany, that initially gave him pause for thought. His and Christopher Isherwood's decision to settle in America in 1939 had been widely denounced in Britain. Their detractors included such as Harold Nicolson – who, by a neat twist of fate, would prove to be Auden's principal opponent in the battle for the Oxford Professorship – and Evelyn Waugh, in whose *Put Out More Flags* two lily-livered left-wing writers, Parsnip and Pimpernell, abscond to America the moment war breaks out. Indeed Auden and Isherwood's dereliction of national duty was even discussed in Parliament, where Sir Jocelyn Lucas asked, in June of 1940, if they might be summoned back and enlisted.

In his reply to Starkie, Auden cautiously pointed out that he was now an American citizen, which was likely to prove a 'fatal handicap' in the election; and, further, that as the post paid only £300 a year, and required long periods of residence in England, it would severely straiten his circumstances. His main source of income during this period was literary journalism for publications such as *The New Yorker* and *The New York Times*, temporary academic appointments, and poetry tours like that commemorated in 'On the Circuit' of 1963:

> Another morning comes: I see,
> Dwindling below me on the plane,
> The roofs of one more audience
> I shall not see again.
>
> God bless the lot of them, although
> I don't remember which was which:
> God bless the U.S.A., so large,
> So friendly, and so rich.

Starkie, however, was undeterred. Unlike many in the Oxford humanities faculties, she fervently believed that the Oxford Professor of Poetry should be a practising poet rather than a literary critic. In Auden she felt she'd found a fitting successor to Day-Lewis. She wrote again, and then again to Ischia, and Auden eventually capitulated. She at once undertook to organize his campaign, since it was deemed – and still is – unmannerly for the candidates to promote their own cause with any vigour.

The results were declared on 9 February, 1956: Auden polled 216 votes, Nicolson 192, and the Shakespeare scholar G. Wilson Knight 91. (Since only those with an Oxford MA were allowed to vote, and votes had to be cast in person, turnout in this era was always pretty low. Waugh, unimpressed by the two 'homosexual socialists', commented caustically in his diary: 'I wish I had taken my degree so I might vote for Knight').

Accordingly, in June of 1956 Auden returned to Oxford University, where he'd achieved only a third-class degree, but where his first book of poems had been published 28 years earlier in an edition of 'about 45 copies', printed up on a hand press purchased by Stephen Spender for £7. The composition of his inaugural lecture, which was entitled 'Making, Knowing and Judging', seems to have caused him acute anxiety; while working on it, he confessed to Stephen Spender in a letter of 8 May, he was periodically overcome by 'fits of real blind sweating panic'; 'Why', he asked his old friend, 'are the English so terrifying?'

The question revealingly signals the ambivalent nature of his relationship at this point with his country of birth. It's worth remembering how very much the poetry of the early Auden, starting with those poems printed by Spender back in 1928, derived its energies and imagery from a desire to figure 'the condition of England':

> Go home, now, stranger, proud of your young stock,
> Stranger, turn back again, frustrate and vexed:
> This land, cut off, will not communicate ...

These lines from 'The Watershed', written while he was still an undergraduate, perfectly capture the tensions that would beset this 'stranger' at last returning to his 'stock' in 1956, seventeen years after leaving them, and how nervous and unsure he felt about what lines of communication would now be open between them. In a canny move he decided to end this first lecture by reading a poem by the most English of English writers, and the one, as he often said, who'd had the most influence on his own early development: without the poetry of Thomas Hardy, he noted, before reciting Hardy's wonderful self-elegy, 'Afterwards', 'I should not now be here'. As Edward Mendelson points out in his introduction to this volume of Auden's critical prose, if the audience refused to applaud when their new Professor of Poetry then sat down, they would seem to be snubbing Hardy as well as Auden.

If Hardy was the most inventive and varied prosodist in the history of English poetry, Auden runs him a close second. On the other hand, Hardy's poetry can't really be said to illustrate the ringing affirmation with which Auden concludes the main text of this first lecture:

> Whatever its actual content and overt interest, every poem
> is rooted in imaginative awe ... there is only one thing that
> all poetry must do; it must praise all it can for being and for
> happening.

Should hymns to the creation be what you're after, then Hardy is surely not your man. And I think the term 'imaginative awe' only makes sense in relation to the poetry of Hardy, and that of the early or English Auden too, if we strip the term of any notion of rapture and think of it as describing a position of radical detachment, allowing all to be surveyed as if from the summit of Wessex Heights, or, in Auden's phrase, 'as the hawk sees it or the helmeted airman'.

It was the clinical authority with which Auden diagnosed the ills besetting his country in what might be called Britain's first post-imperial decade, the 1930s, that led so many to figure him as a kind of national prophet of doom. The effect on his contemporaries can perhaps best be summed up by a couple of lines by the poet Charles Madge (who would later co-found Mass Observation): 'there waited for me in the summer morning / Auden, fiercely. I read, shuddered and knew'. The impish William Empson, however, couldn't help poking a little fun at the spectacle of all these ex-public schoolboys collectively revelling in forthcoming apocalypse:

> Waiting for the end, boys, waiting for the end.
> What is there to be or do?
> What's become of me or you?
> Are we kind or are we true?
> Sitting two and two, boys, waiting for the end.
>
> ('Just a Smack at Auden')

It was at least partly to escape from the role of court-poet to the British Left, a role actively assumed in poems such as 'Spain 1937' but also one to an extent thrust upon him, that Auden moved to America, though the principal reason he always gave for his emigration was that he fell in love with Chester Kallman in the course of a trip to New York in 1939.

He also, though, justified his decision to settle there permanently in relation to his poetic ideals and development. In a letter of 16 January 1940 Auden explained to the Classical scholar E.R. Dodds that America would allow him to attempt to live 'deliberately without roots'; 'America may break one completely', he added, 'but the best of which one is capable is more likely to be drawn out of one here than anywhere else'. His aim, in other words, was to become, if such a thing is possible, a post-national poet. The atavistic conflicts at that moment destroying Europe led him to espouse the belief that responsible poetry must free itself from all tribal affiliations; the poet's task, therefore, was to map possible ways of living in an existential void, in the 'age of anxiety', to borrow the title of his long poem of 1947. *The Age of Anxiety* is set in a bar in New York, and its four characters, Malin, Rosetta, Quant and Emble are allegorical representations of the four Jungian categories of Thinking, Feeling, Intuition and Sensation. A bar, Auden explains in the poem's Prologue, is 'an unprejudiced space in which nothing particular ever happens', which is what makes it the perfect setting for a dispassionate study of the search for meaning that deracinated, alienated modern man must undertake.

And yet, despite his conviction that by leaving England he had freed himself from parochial concerns, from the dangers of nationalist fervour and from his own family romance, and thereby made himself into a truly international and contemporary poet, a bit of Auden seems still to have hankered after the approval of the old gang. What else could explain his willingness to heed Dr Starkie's call in the summer of 1955? The dread inspired by the thought of returning to Oxford, Mendelson notes in his introduction, 'unsettled his whole sense of himself and his career'. This dread found its fullest poetic expression in a poem entitled 'There Will Be No Peace', which 'was an attempt', Auden later revealed to the American critic Monroe K. Spears, 'to describe a very unpleasant dark-night-of-the-soul sort of experience which for several months in 1956 attacked me'. Auden pictures himself confronting serried ranks of nameless enemies, 'Beings of unknown number and gender'; all he knows is that they do not like him:

What have you done to them?
Nothing? Nothing is not an answer:
You will come to believe – how can you help it? –
That you did, you did do something;
You will find yourself wishing you could make them laugh,
You will long for their friendship.

There will be no peace.
Fight back, then, with such courage as you have
And every unchivalrous dodge you know of,
Clear in your conscience on this:
Their cause, if they had one, is nothing to them now;
They hate for hate's sake.

As far as the response to his inaugural lecture went, he needn't have worried. The day after he victoriously declared in a letter to Chester: 'Never in my life have I been so terrified, but thanks to Santa Restituta, I had a triumph and won over my enemies'.

But his use of the term 'enemies' and the unsettling paranoia of 'There Will be No Peace' suggest that his return to his alma mater activated, in Mendelson's words 'a sense of dread at an imaginary threat [that] was stronger than any he had felt at any real one'. Certainly Auden was no favourite of the dominant British critic of the 1950s, F.R. Leavis, whose influential magazine *Scrutiny* routinely attacked him as 'adolescent' or 'immature' – code words for gay. There would never be peace between Auden and Leavis. Probably more troubling for him was the defection of young British poets such as Thom Gunn or Philip Larkin, who saw the American Auden as more of a lost leader than an emotionally arrested deviant. In a *Spectator* review of Auden's 1960 collection

Homage to Clio, Larkin imagined a conversation between someone who had read only the later American Auden, and someone who had read only the pre-1940 English Auden: a 'mystifying gap', he suggested,

> would open between them, as one spoke of a tremendously
> exciting English social poet full of energetic unliterary
> knock-about and unique lucidity of phrase, and the other
> of an engaging, bookish, American talent, too verbose to be
> memorable and too intellectual to be moving. And not only
> would they differ about his poetic character: there would be a
> sharp division of opinion about his poetic stature.

'What's Become of Wystan?' was the title of Larkin's review, which, though written more in sorrow than in anger, must have wounded deeply. It is an impressive testimony to Auden's refusal to engage in literary tit-for-tat that when, a few months later, he was asked to review the American edition of Larkin's *The Less Deceived*, he gave the volume an unambiguous thumbs up.

Auden's stint as Oxford Professor of Poetry lasted from 1956 to 1960. After the first year, to cut down on travel, he was permitted to give his stipulated three lectures per year over a few weeks in early summer, rather than one in each of the three academic terms. He also let it be known that he would be available for conversation with young poets from three o'clock every afternoon in the Cadena coffee shop, where he was approached by, among others, the young Gregory Corso, who tried to kiss the hem of his trousers. Auden's advice to all poetic ephebes – advice that can't have made much impression on the free-spirited Corso – was invariably 'Learn everything there is to know about metre'.

Versions of most of his Oxford lectures were collected in his first large-scale collection of criticism, *The Dyer's Hand* of 1962, which takes up about half of this volume. Auden borrowed the title for *The Dyer's Hand* from Shakepeare's sonnet III, in which the poet presents himself apologizing to his beloved for the fact that his lowly birth has forced him to seek his fortune, and make his name, in the public sphere:

> Thence comes it that my name receives a brand,
> And almost thence my nature is subdued
> To what it works in, like the dyer's hand ...

In Auden's case the apology seems to be to poetry itself, to which his commitment might seem diluted by his willingness to turn his hand to the critical prose he had to write to earn a living.

Auden's productivity throughout his working life in both poetry and prose was really quite astonishing, but particularly so during his American years. He treated himself almost like a machine, observing a rigid work schedule, and fuelling himself with Benzedrine, which probably contributed to the way his face so dramatically cragged up in his mid-fifties. He had not only himself to support, but Chester too. Fortunately, he was never short of an opinion, and seems to have been able to churn out review copy relatively painlessly, but a doorstopper such as this has one gasping again at his sheer industry, at the steely will and powers of concentration that enabled him to fulfil the huge number of tasks that editors offered him, and which he accepted in order to subsidize the writing of his poetry in the summer months.

Auden's prose, like his poetry, insistently reveals his compulsion to seek certainties. In *World Within World*

Stephen Spender suggested that 'Auden's life was devoted to an intellectual effort to analyse, explain and dominate his circumstances'; this effort, it seems to me, can be traced in nearly all of his writings. From the outset a didactic, or spoof-didactic, rhetoric permeates his modes of address. While his father was a doctor, both his grandfathers were clergymen, and surely the imaginative force of many of his most powerful early poems derives from the pulpit-like authority with which they deliver gnomic warnings or issue urgent instructions. Although we may not be sure on what grounds his judgements are made, we watch in awe as he decisively separates the sheep from the goats; 'It is time for the destruction of error', he sternly counsels in a poem written when he was only 22:

> The falling leaves know it, the children,
> At play on the fuming alkali-tip
> Or by the flooded football ground, know it –
> This is the dragon's day, the devourer's.

This is from the poem, later called '1929', that calls for 'the death of the old gang', who are to be 'forgotten in the spring, / The hard bitch and the riding master, / Stiff underground'. Against them he poises a mythical young male redeemer-figure: 'deep in clear lake / The lolling bridegroom, beautiful, there'.

In later life his need to 'dominate his circumstances' drove him to develop various elaborate systems of classification. In many of the pieces collected here divisions and sub-divisions proliferate. This can occasionally make for a somewhat dry reading experience for those not in thrall to the urge to categorize – here is a typical extract from an essay called 'The

Virgin & the Dynamo' included in *The Dyer's Hand*:

> Since all human experience is that of conscious persons, man's
> realization that the World of the Dynamo exists in which events
> happen of themselves and cannot be prevented by anyone's art,
> came later than his realization that the World of the Virgin
> exists. Freedom is an immediate datum of consciousness.
> Necessity is not.
>
> *The Two Chimerical Worlds*
>> (1) The magical polytheistic nature created by the
>> aesthetic illusion which would regard the world of
>> masses as if it were a world of faces. The aesthetic
>> religion says prayers to the Dynamo.
>> (2) The mechanical history created by the scientific
>> illusion which would regard the world of faces as if it
>> were a world of masses. The scientific religion treats
>> the Virgin as a statistic. 'Scientific' politics is animism
>> stood on its head.

More than once, reading these essays, I was put in mind of
Samuel Beckett's parody of philosophical academic discourse
in Lucky's great speech in *Waiting for Godot*. This compulsion
to classify reaches its apogee in an elaborate table that he
includes in an introduction to *Romeo and Juliet*, which offers
the reader four headings: *Character*, *Wrong Choice*, *Consequence*,
and *Right Choice*:

> *Character*: The Apothecary
> *Wrong Choice*: Sells poison to Romeo.
> *Consequence*: Romeo's temptation to suicide is strengthened by
> his possession of the means.

Right Choice: He should have obeyed the law and refused to sell Romeo the poison.

Character: Romeo
Wrong Choice: Kills himself.
Consequence: He is damned.
Right Choice: Even if Juliet had really been dead, he should, at whatever cost of suffering, have remained alive and true to her memory.

Character: Juliet
Wrong Choice: Kills herself.
Consequence: She is damned.
Right Choice: She should have remained alive and true to Romeo's memory.

The final verdict that Auden delivers in this essay on the lovers' suicides struck me as somewhat harsh: 'To kill oneself for love is, perhaps, the noblest act of vanity, but vanity it is, death for the sake of making *una bella figura*'. In a piece on *Othello* he reveals himself similarly unimpressed by the love of the tragedy's principals; he dismisses Desdemona as 'a silly schoolgirl' and tells us he shares Iago's doubts 'as to the durability of the marriage' she has entered into. Surely both *Romeo and Juliet* and *Othello* become rather pointless when perceived from such angles; if we don't feel something valuable and unique has been destroyed when Shakespeare's lovers come to grief, haven't we been wasting our time?

Such judgements reflect the stern, anti-romantic side of Auden, and indeed, as Mendelson argues in his introduction, notions of responsibility and guilt dominate his critical prose in this era. He responded enthusiastically to Edmund Wilson's

Apologies to the Iroquois of 1960, lambasting the 'cultural conceit' that allowed the white man to believe that 'any individual or society that does not share our cultural habits is morally and mentally deficient – it makes no difference if the habit in question is monogamy or a liking for ice cream'. While the most outrageous of the crimes committed against the original inhabitants of America may be in the past, the 'cultural conceit', Auden argues, remains.

As well as *The Dyer's Hand* this volume contains almost one hundred miscellaneous pieces – reviews, radio talks, forewords to the Yale Younger Poets Series that Auden edited (choices from this period included James Wright, William Dickey and John Hollander), essays he wrote for the two book-clubs he worked on with Jacques Barzun and Lionel Trilling, and introductions to various anthologies such as *A Treasure Chest of Tales: A Collection of Great Stories for Children* and *The Viking Book of Aphorisms* (co-edited with Louis Kronenberger). One gets Auden's take on a vast range of writers: Tolkein, Walter de la Mare, Sydney Smith, D.H. Lawrence, Dostoyevsky, Cavafy (one of the best pieces), Firbank (another good one), Byron, Ibsen, Dag Hammarskjöld, Faulkner, Marianne Moore, Robert Frost, Robert Graves, Charles Williams, Martin Luther, Henry Treece, Stendhal, and Van Gogh – plus composers such as Beethoven, Berlioz, Mozart, Stravinsky and Rossini. All these – and many, many more – find their respective niches in the great many-branched Auden schema.

In the process one learns a great deal about all sorts of things, but one also reads a lot of sentences that begin 'There are three kinds of ...' I confess I found it something of a relief to turn from this encyclopedic tome to the ludic, genial, avuncular world of his poems from this period,

MARK FORD

with their twinkle-eyed mix of the arcane and the demotic: 'Steatopygous [large-buttocked], sow-dugged', begins 'Dame Kind', a ripely camp address to Nature, to whom Auden then snuggles up as if he were back in the nursery – 'She mayn't be all She might be but / She *is* our Mum'. The year after his accession to the Oxford Professorship of Poetry he was awarded the Antonio Feltrinelli Foundation prize, which was worth over $33,000. He used a portion of this unexpected windfall to purchase a small farmhouse in Kirchstetten, a village about half an hour by car from Vienna. This signalled the end of his summers in Ischia, a move commemorated in 'Good-Bye to the Mezzogiorno', a poem that typifies the deft, conversational mode that was the later Auden's ideal:

> Out of a gothic North, the pallid children
> > Of a potato, beer-or-whisky
> Guilt culture, we behave like our fathers and come
> > Southward into a sunburnt otherwhere
>
> Of vineyards, baroque, *la bella figura*,
> > To these feminine townships where men
> Are males, and siblings untrained in a ruthless
> > Verbal in-fighting as it is taught
>
> In Protestant rectories upon drizzling
> > Sunday afternoons ...

It's a style he developed most brilliantly in the early 'Letter to Lord Byron', and while his later deployments of it tend to lack the *sprezzatura* of that masterpiece, it yet generates many skilful, amusing poems, and is put to particularly effective use in the sequence 'Thanksgiving for a Habitat', begun in the spring of 1962. Given the fact he was one of the most famous poets on the planet, and at a time when the prestige of poetry was much higher than it is now (*Time* magazine planned to run a cover story on him in 1963, backing out only when the managing editor found out he was gay), it is touching to find him amazed at the turn of fortune that has granted him his own 'bailiwick', and at last luxuriating in the security of home-ownership:

> what I dared not hope or fight for
> is, in my fifties, mine, a toft-and-croft
> where I needn't, ever, be at home *to*
>
> those I am not at home *with*

Many of the poems of this period celebrate friendships; each of the rooms in 'Thanksgiving for a Habitat' is dedicated to a particular friend or couple: Isherwood gets the toilet ('this white-tiled cabin / Arabs call *The House where / Everybody goes*'), Kallman the living room, where he and Auden are comfortably pictured at work on British crossword puzzles under the benign regards of Strauss and Stravinsky, and Louis MacNeice the study, or 'Cave of Making'. Ensconsed in this room where 'neither lovers nor / maids are welcome', Auden sits at his Olivetti Portable, dictionaries ('the very / best money can buy') at hand, turning 'silence' into 'objects'; and in the crafting of these objects, however low their poetic pressure, his pride is undimmed, for 'even a limerick', he declares, 'ought to be something a man of / honor, awaiting death from cancer or a firing-squad, / could read without contempt'.

New York Review of Books (2011)

Review of *The Complete Works of W.H. Auden: Prose, Volume IV, 1956-1962*
edited by Edward Mendelson (Princeton University Press)

A.S.J. Tessimond and Bernard Spencer

When he was twenty-three A.S.J. Tessimond (Arthur Seymour John, Jack to his family, but known as John in later life) wrote to Ezra Pound, who had recently settled in Rapallo, Italy, enclosing some poems and a critical article on George Bernard Shaw. Tessimond's letter does not survive, but Pound's reply does. 'Dear Sir', he wrote,

> If you were in the least familiar with my work you wd. know what I think of criticism in general & not try to arouse my interest with a perfectly innocuous specimen of same. Also you wd. know that I think Shaw simple shit, with no base, and not pick that particular bit of revery. Of course I think all England chiefly shit, and none of Shaw's generation capable of serious thought, or even mental honesty.

If Tessimond wants to be a poet, Pound advises him, he should get out of England, which is 'gone to hell, pustulent etc.' and offers 'nothing but carion [sic] and pus'. He found Tessimond's poems uninspiring ('impression of yr. work neutral'), but he did furnish the young poet with the addresses of a number of magazines in America and Europe, and one of these, *This Quarter*, based in Paris, did publish a few years later 'A painting by Seurat', which was among the batch submitted by Tessimond to *il miglior fabbro* for comment. On the back of the letter Pound scrawled in pencil, 'Not hopeless if you are less than 21'.

Tessimond and Bernard Spencer both died just under 50 years ago, in 1962 and 1963 respectively, and over that half-century their work has attracted flickering rather than sustained attention. This is the third posthumous collection of Spencer's poetry, though the first to reprint his translations, and co-translations (with Lawrence Durrell and Nanos Valaoritis) of George Seferis, Odysseus Elytis and Eugenio Montale. Hubert Nicholson, Tessimond's executor, put together two posthumous selections that included a number of uncollected and unpublished poems (*Not Love Perhaps...* (1978) and *Morning Meeting* (1980)), and then a *Collected Poems* in 1985, handsomely designed by students in the Department of Typography & Graphic Communication at the University of Reading, whose press, Whiteknights, published the book; it is now reissued as a joint venture by Whiteknights and Bloodaxe.

Pound always rather prided himself on being 'out of key with his time', to quote from the first line of 'Hugh Selwyn Mauberley', and in his letter to Tessimond he observes that the young poet 'must be very much out of the world to have invoked me ... from oltre tomba'. Tessimond's neglect, both in his lifetime and since, is generally put down to his being 'out of step with his contemporaries', as the jacket copy to this volume puts it, the contemporaries cited here being Pound, Eliot and Auden. Certainly he never really sounds like Pound or Eliot, despite a brief early fling with Imagism, and a number of poems about cats, and he lacks Auden's intellectual scope and ambition, but he does have a certain amount in common with the Auden of the more occasional pieces, in particular the choruses and songs composed for various film and theatre projects in the 1930s.

Tessimond was born in Birkenhead in 1902 into a relatively prosperous middle-class family; his father was a bank inspector. Like an earlier oddball of British poetry, Thomas Lovell Beddoes, he was sent to Charterhouse School; he can't, however, have enjoyed his time there much, for when he was sixteen he ran away to London, naively hoping to establish himself as a freelance journalist. This bid for independence lasted all of two weeks, after which he let himself be 'trotted back to Birkenhead', as he put it in a letter recounting the episode to Nicholson. On graduating from Liverpool University in the early 1920s he tried his hand at school teaching, but didn't like it, and then moved to London where he worked in various bookshops. Eventually he found a congenial métier in the capital as an advertising copywriter.

Two posthumously published poems present antithetical perspectives on his chosen profession: in 'The ad-man', the negative one, he attacks 'this trumpeter of nothingness', 'this mind for hire, this mental prostitute', who takes the

> True, honourable, honoured, clear and clean,
> And leaves them shabby, worn, diminished, mean.

But in 'Defence of the ad-man' he suggests advertising can be seen as performing a positive, even curative role by ministering to the disappointments of the era and the individual:

> With permitted dope
> He medicines the sickness of our age;
> Offers the ugly, glamour, the hopeless, hope.

It's interesting to compare these pieces to Philip Larkin's advertising poems, such as 'Sunny Prestatyn' or 'Send No Money', or 'Essential Beauty' with its ambivalent response to the vast billboards that 'Screen graves with custard, cover slums with praise / Of motor-oil and cuts of salmon'; these are perfect pictures, Larkin sternly counsels, 'of how life should be', but isn't, for in life nothing's 'new or washed quite clean', and the glamorous girl beckoning us seductively on turns out to be a harbinger of death.

Tessimond published only three collections in his lifetime, *The walls of glass* in 1934, *Voices in a giant city* in 1947, and *Selection* in 1958. The opening poem of *The walls of glass* is called 'Any man speaks'; this any man is not, however, entirely generic, for we learn he lives in London ('To come round the corner of Wardour Street into the Square' [ie. Soho Square]), and that his words belong to a 'dialect shared by you, but not you and you'. Tessimond's idiom is remarkably free of poeticisms and literary affectations from the outset, and the poetic persona offered in this unrhymed sonnet somewhat resembles that of Larkin in his wry acceptance of, and performance of, his own ineptitude:

> I, fulcrum of levers whose ends I cannot see …
> Have this one deftness – that I admit undeftness:
> Know that the stars are far, the levers long:
> Can understand my unstrength.

The deftness of the verse – for almost every poem Tessimond wrote seems to me elegantly turned and surefooted, unerring in its choice of form, vocabulary, rhythm and image – is implicitly presented as compensation for the mess or 'unstrength' or 'undeftness' of his living. Nicholson tells us that Tessimond felt 'misunderstood and unloved by his parents', and that it was 'to his feeling of being starved of maternal affection that psychiatrists later attributed his sexual difficulties, a diagnosis that did nothing to effect a cure'. His sessions with four or five different analysts may not have helped him much, but they certainly generated a number of good poems, such as 'The psychiatrist's song', 'The psychiatrist speaks', and 'The psycho-analyst'; in the last of these the analyst is figured as embodying, like advertising, an enchanting but unreachable world beyond mess and 'undeftness':

> His fees are large, his cares are light,
> His analytic eyes are bright,
> He glows with pride as well he might.
>
> The analyst is always right.

Although a number of Tessimond poems begin 'I am' (nine to be precise), his work is rarely directly autobiographical. These 'I am' poems are nearly all attempts to capture the lives of various city types – a man in a bowler hat, a prostitute, a jack-the-lad – or explore the institutions that shape daily living: 'I am your master and your master's master' ('Money'); 'I am the fairy-tale, the lovely lie, the brighter-than-truth' ('Hollywood'):

> I am the echoing rock that sends you back
> Your own voice grown so bold that with surprise
> You murmur, 'Ah, how sensible I am –
> The plain bluff man, the enemy of sham –
> How sane, how wise!'
> I am the mirror where your image moves,
> Neat and obedient twin, until one day
> It moves before you move; and it is you

Who have to ape its moods and motions, who
Must now obey.

That's Tessimond's take on the popular press, and like his
poems on advertising and money and the silver screen and
the various urban characters who feature in his album of
urban living, it reveals him as an astute and eloquent observer
of the ways in which the culture and institutions of the
day shape the individual, though all the while fostering an
illusion of autonomy and choice. While only occasionally a
topical political poet – most notably in the McSpaundayish
'England (Autumn 1938)' – his work yet presents a telling
and unillusioned analysis of the workings of mid-century
capitalism: 'I am the moving belt you cannot turn from', he
observes in 'Money', 'The threat behind the smiling of the
clock'. Another poem on his own trade, 'Advertising', bleakly
but clear-sightedly acknowledges:

> I am the voice that bids you spend to save and save to spend,
> But always spend that wheels may never end
> Their turning and by turning let you spend to save
> And save to spend, world without end, cradle to grave.

Tessimond can't be said to have developed in any clearly
discernible way as a poet, and it's not easy when reading his
posthumously published poems to decide which is early,
which middle, and which late. All seem buoyed up by his wit
and curiosity and compassion; this is especially surprising
given the fact that in middle age he became severely manic-
depressive, and eventually underwent extensive electric shock
therapy treatment.

He had an odd war; worried that if conscripted he
would not only be 'intensely miserable' but might well prove

'useless and even dangerous to others', he again went on the run, though by now he was nearing forty, abandoning his flat and job and living for a spell incognito with friends. At length he agreed to submit to an army medical, at which, to no one's amazement but his own, the doctors declared him unfit for service.

In 'Any man speaks' Tessimond describes himself as not only 'strangely undeft, bereft', but as 'searching always / For my lost rib'. On his mother's death in 1942 he inherited around £7,000, half of which he spent, in a suitably bi-polar way, on nightclub hostesses, striptease girls and models, while half went on his doomed attempt to cure himself through analysis. He talked often, Nicholson reports, of suicide, but never actually attempted it; his hilarious 'Letter from Luton' – which seems to me much funnier than John Betjeman's 'Slough' – gives a vivid snapshot of his inner unhappiness, and the humour with which he defied it:

Dear Hubert,

Bored, malevolent and mute on
A wet park seat, I look at life and Luton
And think of spittle, slaughterhouses, double
Pneumonia, schizophrenia, kidney trouble,
Piles, paranoia, gallstones in the bladder,
Manic depressive madness growing madder,
Cretins with hideous tropical diseases
And red-eyed necrophiles – while on the breezes
From Luton Gasworks comes a stench that closes
Like a damp frigid hand on my neuroses,
And Time (arthritic deaf-mute) stumbles on
And on and on and on.

Yours glumly,

John

He died shortly before his sixtieth birthday of a brain haemorrhage, possibly induced by his extensive ect sessions; it was two days before his body was found in his flat in Chelsea. Nicholson tells us in his introduction that Tessimond fell in love often and unsuitably, experiencing 'a long succession of never wholly consummated passions'. Yet his poems rarely convey the yearnings of a deluded romantic; a four-line poem dedicated to one J.M. titled 'In that cold land' movingly suggests it was really companionship rather than sexual bliss that he sought in his efforts to recover his lost rib:

> Ghosts do not kiss, or, if they kiss, they feel
> > Ice touching ice, and turn away, and shiver;
> But there as here, perhaps, we still can steal
> > Quietly off, and talk and talk for ever.

Like Tessimond, Bernard Spencer published only three books in his lifetime: *Aegean Islands and Other Poems* in 1946; his collaborative translations of the poetry of George Seferis in 1948; and a second volume of his own work, *With Luck Lasting*, in 1963. His origins were somewhat grander than Tessimond's. He was born in 1909 in Madras, India, the second son of Sir Charles Gordon Spencer, a high court judge there. After a series of threatening infant illnesses, he was sent back when only eighteen months old to England to be brought up by relatives. Spencer and his siblings can have seen little of their parents while growing up, and it is interesting to note that in the poem 'My Sister', the death of Sir Charles functions as a mere backdrop to memories of his early life with his sister Cynthia. At Marlborough he was in the same year as Anthony Blunt, and just junior to Louis MacNeice and John Betjeman. Among his friends at Oxford were Isaiah Berlin, Maurice

Bowra and Stephen Spender, with whom he co-edited the magazine *Oxford Poetry* in 1930.

In his excellent introduction to this definitive *Complete Poetry*, Peter Robinson characterizes Spencer as an unconfident poet who, when his luck was in, wrote poems that were 'profoundly uncertain': 'Within his small *oeuvre*, poem after poem sounds true. That sound sense of reliable poetry was achieved under the shadow of an urge to doubt the entire business'. He was 'delightful humorous company', Betjeman reflected in an article on MacNeice and Spencer published in *London Magazine* shortly after their deaths, eight days apart, in September of 1963, but 'diffident about his own work … I should think a rejection slip would have set him back for years'. Diffidence is not a quality one associates with the dominant poet of the 1930s, W.H. Auden, and Spencer, like so many of his generation, first had to fight his way clear of the Audenesque:

> White factories lancing sky
> As the city grew near
> Were symbols of changed state,
>
> Pulse and strength of steel arms
> Seemed hammering out new world
> Not by you informed.

This is the opening of a poem called 'Poem' that was published in *Oxford Poetry* in 1931, and reveals little beyond how very quickly Auden, whose first commercial book, *Poems*, had appeared only the year before, had transformed the concept and language of poetry for his contemporaries. Spencer's early efforts are mainly in this mode. A short but extremely telling note on Auden that he wrote for the November 1937 Auden special issue of *New Verse* (on which he was working as an editorial assistant to Geoffrey Grigson at the time, and where most of his own early work appeared), implies that as the 1930s progressed, Spencer slowly came to realize that Auden was not so much the charismatic leader whose example he should follow, but his poetic antithesis: 'He succeeds', this note concludes, 'in brutalizing his thought and language to the level from which important poetry proceeds'.

It was Edward Thomas, like Spencer a profound self-doubter, whose work suggested how he might move away from the urgent, gnomic compressions of Wystan the wunderkind. 'In what sense am I joining in?' he asks in the opening poem, 'Allotments: April', of his first collection; it is Spencer's sense of being at an oblique angle to the scene or characters that he describes that most allies his poetry with that of Thomas, who time and again dramatized his inability to bite the day to its core.

Yet while Thomas's poethood was fundamentally bound up with the history and fate of England (and Wales), Spencer only really came into his own after he began living abroad as a lecturer for the newly founded British Council. His first appointment was as a teacher and librarian at the Institute of English studies in Salonika in Greece; there followed six years in Cairo (1940-46), where he met Keith Douglas and Ruth Speirs, the brilliant translator of the poems of Rilke, and edited the magazine *Personal Landscape* with Lawrence Durrell and Robin Fedden. Later postings included Palermo, Turin, Athens, Madrid (twice), Ankara and Vienna, where he died in 1963 in somewhat mysterious circumstances.

'My end of Europe is at war', begins 'Salonika June 1940'. The town would be shelled in earnest a few months later by the invading Italians. 'Not by this brilliant bay', Spencer coolly observes,

> Nor in Hampstead now where leaves are green,
> Any more exists a word or a lock which gunfire may not break,
> Or a love whose range it may not take.

Yet his dominant response to the impending brutalities was to find ways of *not* brutalizing thought and language in an attempt to write 'important poetry'. His poems, he insisted to Alan Ross, are 'always factual'; but that's not to imply that there is anything merely journalistic about them. For the facts are marshalled not only to preserve the contingencies of the scene Spencer presents, but as vertical time probes into the larger contingencies of memory and history.

In the poem 'In Athens', from the mid-1950s, he passes on the street a stranger who looks familiar:

> The knock inside your chest:
> someone you loved was like her; there is given
> neither name nor time, except it was long ago:
> the scene, half caught, then blurred;
> a village on the left perhaps, fields steeply rising.

Nothing more emerges of the primal memory the stranger evokes, but how typical, he notes, of 'the twist in the plotting of things' that it should happen in Athens,

> so near where they talked well on love
> two civilisations ago, and found
> splendid and jeering images: horses plunging,
> the apple cut, the Hidden One.

A wryness,
and a name your body is trying to make you hear ...

Historical knowledge and the quest for the vanished name buried somewhere in his own body 'twist' together to induce a haunting awareness of relation and disconnection, a sense of the mixture of coincidence and helplessness, of pattern and randomness that his oeuvre as a whole renders with such fidelity and precision. 'Letter Home', written in Franco's Madrid in the early 1950s, concludes with a similar braiding together of the personal and the historical to create another delicate moment of 'wryness', as the poet pursues his self-doubt into a state of acute, almost visionary unconfidence:

> the heat follows me around
> like an overcoat in a dream; a ship's siren from the river
> trembles the air with sorrows and names of iron harbours.
> City where I live, not home, road that flowers with police,
> what in all worlds am I doing here?

Spencer was married twice: his first wife (of eleven years), Nora, died of tuberculosis in 1947, and Spencer commemorated their life together in a beautiful elegy, 'At Courmayeur'. The following year he was diagnosed with the same disease, and sought treatment in a hospital in Switzerland. (His health seems always to have been somewhat precarious owing to a congenital heart condition). 'We lie here', he observed about his stay in the Beau-Soleil clinic in Leysin, 'in our similar rooms with the white / furniture, with our bit of Death inside us'. In his bare white room he searches for 'some link, some link', to connect him to the outside world. The operation, a thoracotomy, was a success.

In 1961 Spencer married again, in Madrid. The tiny poem 'Morning in Madrid' may be an oblique aubade to the new life he was about to embark on – or it may be just a delightful bit of scene-painting:

> Skirmish of wheels and bells and someone calling:
> a donkey's bronchial greeting, groan and whistle,
> the weeping factory sirens rising, falling.
>
> Yelping of engines from the railyard drifted:
> then, prelude to the gold-of-wine of morning,
> the thunderstorm of iron shutters lifted.

From Madrid he was transferred to Vienna, where he became a father at the age of 53. That same year his second collection, *With Luck Lasting*, was published by Hodder and Stoughton, and was chosen as that summer's Poetry Book Society Recommendation. But Spencer's luck, it soon transpired, was about to give out. He fell ill in the course of a holiday to the Adriatic; on his return to Vienna he entered a clinic to get his condition investigated, but under circumstances that have never been properly explained, he was allowed to leave the clinic on the evening of 10 September – or perhaps in a deluded state he managed to flee from it. His body was discovered early the next morning beside a suburban railway line, with head injuries suggesting he'd been hit by a train.

In what was probably his last poem, addressed to the infant Piers Spencer, aged five months old, he imagines his son following in his father's footsteps and becoming a poet, and so being short of money; nevertheless, though his profession will scare off some, others

> will edge your way, and speculate
> how if they could get closer somehow and overhear,
> they might learn something that would make them rich.

Like Tessimond, Spencer wrote a number of poems about money ('Most things have a market price...', 'Behaviour of Money'); neither had the self-belief or ambition or fertility of invention to attempt careers as professional poets in the mode of Pound or Eliot or Auden, and neither attempted to write 'important poetry', nor ever thought to support themselves, let alone get literally rich, from their work. This makes them, I suppose, 'lesser artists', to borrow the title of a Tessimond poem on just this subject, but not all good poetry is also 'important poetry'. It is wonderful to have these two elegant and original poets back in print, for both indubitably belong, in Tessimond's words, to that

> Unsatisfied, unsatisfiable crew
> Whom the ironical gods in a casual moment
> Chose for their gift of tongues and touched with fire.

London Review of Books (2011)

Review of A.S.J. Tessimond's *Collected Poems* edited by Hubert Nicholson (Bloodaxe / Whiteknights Press) and Bernard Spencer's *Complete Poetry, Translations & Selected Prose* edited by Peter Robinson (Bloodaxe)

Child Randall

Born in 1914, Randall Jarrell belonged to the first generation of American poets who found a ready home in the country's burgeoning university system. Of the great modernists of the previous era, only Robert Frost assumed the role of pedagogue to undergraduates, taking his first job at Amherst College in 1917. Pound, Eliot, Wallace Stevens, William Carlos Williams, Marianne Moore, Hart Crane, all lived by other means; though it's worth pointing out that the poetry and criticism of Eliot in particular, and of Pound to a lesser extent, played a significant role in shaping the curriculum and methodologies these expanding departments adopted. Certainly those that fell under the sway of the New Critics, who took so many of their cues from Eliot, liked to present literary history as culminating in *The Waste Land*, a poem that required their expert professional guidance to be understood.

Jarrell once planned a study of Eliot that would have cut decisively across the grain of New Critical source-hunting and explorations of Eliot's use of Grail mythology or Wagner or the Fisher King of the kind one finds in Cleanth Brooks 1939 study of the poet. *T.S. Eliot and Obsessional Neurosis,* Jarrell planned to call it, and one can surmise the argument he intended to make from the paragraph he devotes to Eliot in a lecture of 1962 called 'Fifty Years of American Poetry'. 'Won't the future', Jarrell exclaims,

> say to us in helpless astonishment: 'But did you actually believe
> that all those things about objective correlatives, classicism,

the tradition, applied to *his* poetry? Surely you must have seen
that he was one of the most subjective and daemonic poets
who ever lived, the victim and helpless beneficiary of his own
inexorable compulsions, obsessions? From a psychoanalytical
point of view he was far and away the most interesting poet of
your century. But for you, of course, after the first few years,
his poetry existed undersea, thousands of feet below that deluge
of exegesis, explication, source listing, scholarship, and criticism
that overwhelmed it. And yet how bravely and personally it
survived, its eyes neither coral nor mother-of-pearl but plainly
human, full of human anguish!'

Once you start quoting from Jarrell's essays, it's hard to stop.
Such a passage exemplifies many of his virtues as a critic: his
urgency, his unstuffiness, his mixing of the colloquial and
the rhapsodic, his daring ('human anguish!'), his scorn for
orthodoxy and jargon, his indifference to cliques and party-
lines, his unwavering trust in his own intuitions. Jarrell spent
nearly all his adult life in academic departments whose raison
d'être was the professionalization of responses to literature,
and yet managed to retain the power to read, and to talk about
his reading, with the wide-eyed excitement of a child.

'Child Randall', Lowell addresses him, inevitably, in
the second of his sonnets for Jarrell, the one that restages his
friend's peculiar death (Jarrell was sideswiped by a car in the
course of an evening walk):

> black-gloved, black-coated, you plod out stubbornly
> as if in lockstep to grasp your blank not-I
> at the foot of the tunnel … as if asleep, Child Randall,
> greeting the cars, and approving – your harsh luminosity.

It was never decisively established whether or not he intended
to commit suicide, but the coroner decided it was an accident.
While the premature deaths of such as John Berryman and
Delmore Schwartz and Sylvia Plath seemed somehow implicit
in the trajectory of their careers, there was nothing remotely
maudit about Jarrell, until the last couple of years of his life,
when the approach of his fiftieth birthday induced a bout
of what he called, after Freud, *torschlusspanik* – door-closing
panic. This led to the prescription of a drug that converted his
depression into manic fits of elation, erratic behaviour – on
one occasion he tried to tip a waitress $1,500 – hospitalization,
the slashing of a wrist, and his lonely, ambiguous death at the
edge of a road near Chapel Hill in North Carolina, at the age
of 51.

Children abound in Jarrell's poetry. '90 North',
one of his earliest successful poems, opens with a sick child
imagining a heroic voyage to the North Pole, then cuts to the
adult, actually at the North Pole, disappointed, as romantics
must always be, by the gap between fantasy and reality. The
flag he has planted 'snaps in the glare and silence', and all the
explorer who has at last fulfilled his dream can think is, 'And
now what? Why, go back'. Another poem from the same
period, 'Children Selecting Books in a Library', celebrates the
pact made by all book-lovers, who live 'By trading another's
sorrow for our own; another's / Impossibilities, still unbelieved
in, for our own'. The child reader is figured in a state of 'blind
grace', a phrase that seems to me to capture perfectly the effect
of Jarrell's criticism at its most potent, as in the discussion of
Eliot quoted above, for instance, or in his extended dissection
of Robert Frost's 'Home Burial'. This gripping 25-page essay
manages, through pure instinct, to irradiate every aspect of
the poem's workings, and to make the reader experience to

the full each carefully nuanced horror of the psychological torment Frost's warring couple inflict upon each other. It's Jarrell's most impressive feat of sustained close reading, and if asked to mount a defence of criticism, it would, I think, be among the first of the pieces that I'd summon to the witness stand.

Jarrell's criticism has never, of course, lacked advocates or admirers; as well as inspiring an interest in poetry in a wide and general readership, it played a major role in establishing or consolidating the reputations of many of the twentieth-century poets whose work has survived best. Jarrell, to put it simply, had great taste in poetry, and an infectious enthusiasm when he wrote or talked about it.

His own poetry, however, has fared less well. His habit of making sick children or unstable, often marginalized women the subjects or narrators of his poems has led to numerous charges of sentimentality, and it seems that his first – or possibly only – suicide attempt was in part prompted by a particularly vicious review in the *New York Times* of his final, and most child-saturated collection, *The Lost World* (1965); this review accused him of 'doddering infantilism', 'of familiar, clanging vulgarity, corny clichés, cutenesses', and poured scorn on 'the intolerable self-indulgence of his tear-jerking, bourgeois sentimentality'. On the other hand, in recent years Jarrell's concern for the helpless or voiceless or overlooked has elicited from critics such as Stephen Burt and Langdon Hammer and James Longenbach favourable comparisons with the predatory, will-to-power poetics of Lowell, or the rampant self-aggrandizing confessionalism of Berryman and Plath.

Assessments of Jarrell as a poet inevitably play him off against his mid-century peers, either lamenting, or lauding, the absence of the combination of ruthlessness and brinkmanship that led to the 'breakthroughs' made in volumes such as *Life Studies* or *Ariel* or *77 Dream Songs*. Certainly he lacked Lowell's or Plath's gift for the deadly, single phrase, though he liked to try to end his poems with some grand-sounding, abstract truth: 'but, alas, eternity!' or 'I, I, the future that mends everything'. And yet, as Michael Hofmann has argued, Jarrell the poet is really at his most original when at his most wayward and leisurely, in prolix, rambling pieces like 'The End of the Rainbow', which presents the life of an ageing New England-born landscape painter called Content; Content has settled in California where she runs a shop and lives with a succession of dogs, all called Su-Su. The poem consists mainly of her indecisive reflections on not having done all that much with her life. Gazing into her mirror, through tears, she says:

> 'Look at my life. Should I go on with it?
> It seems to you I have ... a real gift?
> I shouldn't like to keep on if I only ...
> It seems to you my life is a success?'

> Death answers, *Yes. Well, yes.*

Certainly we're a long way from Lady Lazarus and the art of dying exceptionally well.

Robert Frost's studies of lonely women in poems like 'The Hill Wife' or 'A Servant to Servants' are undoubtedly the poetic progenitors of Jarrell's gallery of unhappy women, whose plight might be summed up by the sigh that concludes the monologue of the middle-aged housewife of 'Next Day': 'I stand beside my grave / Confused with my life, that is commonplace and solitary'. However one responds to the sufferings of Plath or Lowell or Berryman or Sexton, one is unlikely to call them 'commonplace' – unless one really *really* wants to insult them. They, as much as the Beats, thought of themselves as special and different, while Jarrell, though in many ways as singular as any of the pure products of America that went so dramatically crazy, filled his poetry with low-key, average, muted misery, or, on occasion, low-key, average, muted joy: one of his last poems, 'A Man Meets a Woman in the Street', gives us a man pursuing a woman as she walks towards Central Park, catching up with her, then touching her: 'Because, after all, it *is* my wife / In a new dress from Bergdorf's …' It's a good job Joseph Bennett, the *New York Times* critic who savaged *The Lost World*, wasn't able to get his teeth into *this* poem, which was published posthumously.

Jarrell's fascination with the helpless probably had its origins not only in Frost's poems about women, but in his youthful Marxism, and his wide reading in psychoanalytical theory. His characters are disabled either by some kind of primal hang-up, such as fear of sex, which is what warps Content in 'The End of the Rainbow', or by institutions that rob them of all agency. The air force personnel of Jarrell's numerous World War II poems could hardly be more removed from the joyous self-command with which poets like Yeats and Auden invested the romantic figure of the airman, as they pursue through the skies a Nietzschean 'lonely impulse of delight'. Jarrell's wingmen and pilots and bombers and ball turret gunners are tiny cogs in a vast impersonal machine that is utterly indifferent to their lives. It's a point that his most famous poem, the five-line 'The Death of the Ball Turret Gunner' makes in its startling opening line, 'From my mother's sleep I fell into the State', and dramatically enacts in its gruesome final one: 'When I died they washed me out of the turret with a hose'. Life in the army (Jarrell spent three and a half years training pilots at air force bases in Texas, Illinois and Arizona) perfectly illustrated his vision of the individual's alienating subservience to the state; the bulk of army life, he observed in a letter from this period, involves 'passively suffering ... not knowing why anything's happened, helplessly ignorant and determined'. Only sleep and dreams offer his airmen temporary respite from the grinding mechanism of the war.

Jarrell began his only novel, *Pictures from an Institution*, in 1951, and it was published in 1954. The year after he was demobbed he spent a semester teaching at the women's college Sarah Lawrence in Bronxville, New York; one of his colleagues there was Mary McCarthy, who used the experience to write her own campus novel, *The Groves of Academe* (1952). As in his analysis of the army, to which he at one point compares the semi-fictional college of Benton, Jarrell sets out to show how an institution is 'always a man's shadow shortened in the sun' (he's quoting from Emerson here), even if that institution fancies itself a progressive liberal arts college. Jarrell's focus is not, however, on the rank and file, who in this case would be students – they barely appear in the novel – but on the staff, and the genre of his writing switches from sentiment to satire.

Pictures from an Institution not only features a campus with no students, it also has no plot. Its seven linked chapters are really extended portraits of particular faculty members, and their characters were modelled to some degree on real people: the acerbic novelist Gertrude Johnson has long been linked with Mary McCarthy, for instance, and Irene Rosenbaum with Hannah Arendt. The book's self-effacing narrator is a poet who bears a striking resemblance to Jarrell himself. I say 'self-effacing', but he's only that in so far as he takes a backseat in the various scenes the book dramatizes; his descriptions, however, of all those he observes crackle with a wit not dissimilar from that on display in Jarrell's reviews and letters. The book is really an extended sequence of *bons mots*, some quite funny, some less so. We meet the novel's characters pretty much entirely through the prism of the narrator's witticisms: 'Jerrold was almost courtly, like a wooden leg of the old school; Fern smelled, surely, of brimstone and sulphur; and John was like a saint – a saint of the future, perhaps. He was no more trouble around the house than a Field Book of North American Reptiles'. It's probably best read in short bursts, or dipped into, for Jarrell's determination to sparkle at every turn can become a little wearing. Although he published two children's books in the 1960s, illustrated by Maurice Sendak, he never attempted another novel.

Dwight Robbins, the President of Benton, is described as being 'so well adjusted to his environment that sometimes you could not tell which was the environment and which was President Robbins'. Like his creator, Robbins is a wunderkind, President of Benton by the age of 34, and he would have reached this pinnacle by the age of 29 had he not spent his early years pursuing a successful career in diving. Jarrell's animosity towards him is palpable, and perhaps reflects his own anxiety at being so well suited to the academic institutions that nurtured him, and in which he shone. He was spotted as an undergraduate at Vanderbilt by John Crowe Ransom, and he followed his mentor for graduate studies to Kenyon; there he roomed with Lowell in the attic of Ransom's own house, and submitted his thesis on the poetry of A. E. Housman in 1939. That very year he was offered, and accepted, a job at the University of Texas-Austin. By all accounts a superb and charismatic teacher, he once declared he loved teaching so much he'd *pay* to do it! Most of his academic life was spent at the Women's College of North Carolina in Greenboro, though he also had a not particularly happy year at Princeton (1951–52), where he lectured on Auden, remorselessly itemizing the means by which his once great hero had fallen from poetic grace. ('Randall is in love with me', was Auden's witty riposte). Imaginatively and spiritually Jarrell decried institutions, but until his sad and difficult last two years, he operated skilfully and successfully within them, and they in turn treated his talents with respect. No one seems to have complained about his maverick, anti-academic brand of criticism, nor demanded he finish his book on T.S. Eliot for an upcoming tenure review.

'If only, somehow, I had learned to live', laments the narrator of the late poem 'The Player Piano', one of Jarrell's finest. Many of his poetry's characters feel they have missed out on life, or are trying to come to terms with their sense of being superannuated. They long to be transformed – 'You know what I was, / You see what I am: change me, change me!' as the woman at the Washington Zoo bursts out. A related fear about the growing inauthenticity and intellectual decline of American culture stalks the essays Jarrell wrote in the latter part of his career, pieces such as 'The Taste of the Age', or 'A Sad Heart at the Supermarket', in which he complains, a little naïvely, that the trouble with capitalism is that it's all about making people buy things. The same point is made in 'Next Day', which opens in a supermarket. The narrator is trying to choose between detergents:

> Moving from Cheer to Joy, from Joy to All,
> I take a box
> And add it to my wild rice, my Cornish game hens.

Post-war plenty and the expansion of consumer choice
– that wild rice, those Cornish game hens – prove, alas, no
compensation for the indignities of ageing. The boy who
carries the housewife's groceries to the car fails to notice her as
appreciatively as she'd like, and this triggers her descent into
the 'commonplace' self-disgust, the quotidian despair so many
of Jarrell's poems seek to dramatize:

> I am afraid, this morning, of my face.
> It looks at me
> From the rear-view mirror, with the eyes I hate,
> The smile I hate. Its plain, lined look
> Of gray discovery
> Repeats to me: 'You're old.' That's all, I'm old.

London Review of Books (2010)

Review of *Pictures from an Institution* by Randall Jarrell (The University of
Chicago Press)

Joan Murray and the Bats of Wisdom

W.H. Auden spent much of the summer of 1946 in a beach house owned by his friends James and Tania Stern in Cherry Grove on Fire Island, just south of Long Island. He was at work on his long poem *The Age of Anxiety* that would be published the following year; he had also recently been appointed editor of the Yale Series of Younger Poets, taking over from Archibald MacLeish, whose multifarious commitments had meant he could devote little time to rigorous perusal of the manuscripts of first volumes of poems sent on to him by Yale University Press. Auden, then at the height of his prestige, was the first choice of the Yale committee that met on 6 May to decide MacLeish's successor. He accepted in a letter of 10 May, characteristically observing: 'I am not at all sure that a poet is the best judge of his contemporaries, but I'm willing to have a shot at it if you are'. In the event he would edit the series until 1959, and launch the careers of a number of the most important poets of the post-war era: Adrienne Rich (1951), W.S. Merwin (1952), John Ashbery (1956), James Wright (1957), and John Hollander (1958). All had their first books chosen by Auden for publication in the Yale Series of Younger Poets.[1]

None of the 10 manuscripts that Auden took with him to Fire Island in the summer of 1946, however, seemed to him worthy of the accolade. Accordingly he wrote to Eugene

[1] For a fuller account of Auden's editorship of the series see George Bradley's excellent introduction to *The Yale Younger Poets Anthology* (Yale University Press, 1998), pp. lviii-lxii. I am much indebted to Bradley for many details concerning the publication of Murray's work in the series.

MARK FORD

Davidson, the Yale University Press editor in charge of the
series, with a suggestion of his own: 'I have just heard that the
poems of Joan Murray which I told you about are available
and, in my opinion, they are the best we have. May I have
your permission to choose them? She died in 1942 at the age
of 23' (she was in fact 24). Auden knew about Murray's work
because she had been a student of his at the New School some
six years earlier. Although it must have struck Davidson and
his fellow Yale editors as rather odd to make the award, which
was intended to promote 'such verse as seems to give the
fairest promise for the future of American poetry', to quote
from the statement of purpose included in early volumes in
the series, to a dead poet born in London of Canadian parents,
no one at the Press demurred, and *Poems* by Joan Murray,
1917–1942, was duly published in May of 1947, attracting
reviews in papers and journals such as *Poetry*, *The Saturday
Review*, the *New York Times Book Review*, and the *New Yorker*.
William Meredith, who had himself received the prize in
1944 for his first collection, *Love Letter from an Impossible Land*,
acclaimed Murray's 'powerful and distinctive voice' in *Poetry*,
but reported himself puzzled by her 'abrupt transitions from
image to image', transitions 'too quick and often too irrational
for this reader'. Milton Crane in the *New York Times* rather
more harshly described the poems as giving 'the impression
of being unborn'.

The volume came with a Foreword by Auden and
an Editor's Note by Grant Code, a writer and lecturer on
theatre and dance, and founder and manager of the Brooklyn
Museum Dance Center that ran from 1935 to 1938. Code had
not known the dead poet personally, but he was a friend of
Murray's mother, who was a diseuse and moved in theatrical
circles, and he was an occasional dabbler in verse himself (his

work features alongside that of Malcolm Cowley and John Wheelwright in the anthology *Eight More Harvard Poets* of 1923). In his negotiations with Yale Auden declared himself uncomfortable with the notion that each book he selected should be introduced by the editor of the series, complaining: 'These introductions always sound awful, and the whole idea that a new poet should be introduced by an older one as if he were a debutante or a new face cream, deplorable and false'. In his very brief (it runs to a mere page and a half) Foreword to his initial selection he makes exactly this point in his opening paragraph, revealing that his own 'personal response' to a book of poems with an introduction by an older writer 'is a suspicion that the publishers are afraid that the poems are not very good and want reassurance'. Auden, as would become his wont in these introductions, pretty much evades the duty of making a case for Murray's work, limiting himself to a single sentence that attempts to articulate its distinctive qualities: 'In Miss Murray's poetry', he observes (and it's not an observation that gets us very far), 'the dominant emotion is, I think, a feeling of isolation, and her characteristic images tactile shapes which reassure her that "Here" and "There" are both related to each other'. This could surely be applied to any number of volumes of poetry published since the romantics.

The Editor's Note by Grant Code would have indicated to purchasers of the book back in 1947 a rather stronger sense of the unusual nature of Murray's poetry; the only other poet mentioned in Code's Note is Emily Dickinson, and his discussion of his task as Murray's editor inevitably recalls the controversy attending editorial attempts to standardize Dickinson's work. Murray's manuscripts, which were handed over to him by Murray's mother (known as Peggy, her full name being Florence Margaret Toaps Murray) were, he reports, in a state of 'confusion, pages of prose mixed with pages of verse and scarcely two pages of anything together that belonged together': many poems existed in different versions, Murray's spelling was 'capricious', few of the poems were titled, and fewer properly punctuated. Some words were clearly 'makeshift' choices that she intended later to revise, and some downright ungrammatical. He tried to fix most of these, although the book does include the odd verbal peculiarity, such as the last line of 'Sleep, Whose Hour Has Come' that makes a verb into an adjective: 'And sleep is still retribute'. On occasion Code took the liberty of substituting a choice of his own in place of what Murray had written, as when he altered 'connubial' to 'convivial' in line 17 of 'Believe Me, My Fears Are Ancient', on the grounds that the effect of 'connubial' is 'disturbing'. I rather regret this particular editorial decision, since the poem, like a number of Murray's, is about what one might call the procreative urge, 'the burst into spring', and the lines in question depict the human mind casting off gloom and doubts, 'conglomerate mourners', and rejoicing in the desire 'to slip over and be connubial', or as Code would have it 'convivial'. It surely takes an exceptionally sensitive reader to be disturbed by Murray's original choice, which hardly plunges us into the territory of *Lady Chatterley's Lover*.

Code's task in sorting through the material he was given and making from these drafts a publishable book was clearly a formidable one.[2] He evidently smoothed and regularized; he added the word 'Trees' off his own bat to a

---

[2] The trunk containing all of Murray's original manuscripts was lost by removal men, or so it was thought, when her mother sold her daughter's papers, along with her own much more voluminous archives, to Smith College in 1968. However, my inquiries to the current Smith archivist about this lost trunk stimulated a search for it, and I am delighted to report that it has now been found, and is in the process of being catalogued.

poem, without telling us which one (my guess is stanza 4 of 'Spring': 'Sap flies high to the head of tall / Trees in a leaping drunk ...'). He adjusted her syntax and added the occasional 'colorless connective' where he felt it was needed. For titles he normally used the first line, in the mode of Auden's own *Poems* of 1930, but sometimes came up with a descriptive title of his own.

It is easy to deride what John Ashbery has called, in a short piece on Murray published in the *Poetry Project Newsletter* of October / November 2003, these 'ministrations of a well-meaning but somewhat heavy-handed editor'. Code also got increasingly on Auden's wick as work on the book proceeded, although not as much as Peggy, about whom Auden wrote to Davidson at Yale with a word to the wise: 'From what I know of Mama, I would advise you confidentially to deal with her through Mr. Code'. Indeed, Auden also told Davidson that Mrs Murray had once written him a letter accusing him of having killed her daughter! Possibly Murray *mère* attributed her daughter's early death in January of 1942 not to complications deriving from a rheumatic heart condition, but to the compositional fever that her attendance of Auden's lectures on 'Poetry and Culture' at the New School in the autumn of 1940 had inspired. (Much of her oeuvre, it seems, was written in the 16 months left to her after she began taking Auden's course). Code omitted from the book forty poems that he decided were 'incomplete, fragmentary, or immature', but he refused to grant Auden's pleas that he cull still further. He also wanted to include as an appendix a biographical sketch he titled 'A Faun Surmising', made up partly of his observations and speculations, and partly of passages from Murray's letters and diaries. A copy of this survives in the Smith Archives, and I would dearly love to read it. He apparently compiled notes for the poems too. Confronted by this editorial apparatus, Auden firmly drew the line: he instructed Davidson that Code's notes and 'A Faun Surmising' were not to appear in the book 'because – entre nous – they make me very sick'. In his Foreword he sternly insists on the importance of not being 'distracted by sentimental speculation' about the author's life and early death, or what she might have gone on to write.

'Heavy-handed' Code may well, on occasion, have been, but I would like to speak up briefly, before turning to the poems themselves, on his arranging of the volume into seven books, 'grouped', in his words, 'by subject'. Within these books individual pieces are carefully ordered so as to create, where possible, a sense of 'sequence and development of thought running through several poems'. Murray's idiom can seem, as the reviews by such as William Meredith and Milton Crane testify, so mobile, so resistant to attempts to parse it into prose sense, that one can lose sight of the poem's 'subject'. Code, it strikes me, thought long and hard about the best way to bring to the fore Murray's thematic concerns, and his arrangements are both effective and helpful in getting a grip on the volume as a whole. This coherence is stronger in some books than in others: many of the poems in Book One are urban and verging on the satirical, while those in Three deal with nature and rural life (mainly in Vermont); most of those in the short Book Four approach religious issues, whereas those in Six are predominantly concerned with conquest, empire and exile, and those in Seven with mythological figures, from Bast, the Egyptian cat goddess, to Penelope, Ulysses and Orpheus. Two and Five have less distinctive characters, but one gets runs of poems on topics such as art, sleep, and the sea. I wouldn't deny that many of Murray's poems veer hither and thither in all manner of competing directions, skipping from image to image with electrical speed and insouciance, but beneath their hectic surfaces one can often discern a shadowy but purposeful progression of thought and argument.

Among the items listed in her section of the Murray archives at Smith is an edition of J.B. Leishman's 1941 Hogarth Press edition of Rainer Maria Rilke's *Selected Poems*. If Auden was evidently the primary and fundamental catalyst for Murray's sudden and startling poetic 'burst into spring', it was the Rilke-influenced strand of Auden found throughout *Poems*, and in parts of *The Orators* (1932) and *Look, Stranger!* (1936), rather than the political or journalistic or camp or comic or moralistic aspects of his work, that Murray appropriated, and developed into a medium of her own. Auden's influence, it's worth stressing at this point, was everywhere in the poetry that was being written in the late thirties and early forties both in Britain and America, from Philip Larkin to John Berryman, from Stephen Spender to Delmore Schwartz, from Nicholas Moore to Elizabeth Bishop and Randall Jarrell. Murray homed in on the cryptic, elliptical idiom that dominates Auden's first Faber collection, as the first piece in her own *Poems* rather too graphically demonstrates. It consists of three ABAB rhyming quatrains:

> If, here in the city, lights glare from various source,
> Look out of the window, thin-faced man.
> Three portent cities repeat the pattern and the course
> That history ran.

> Three slender veins, clotted and ambiguous,
> Are those inlocked hands.
> Three startled cries now rise incredulous,
> Where once sprang barren sands.

Give back night to receding sky.
Let stars (the things that remain)
Orbit their quiet to the lie
That is here city and various city pain.

The noun 'portent' in line 3 has been weirdly wrenched into use as an adjective, as if the course of history were insisting that there wasn't time for the —ous to be added to it, or for a more meaningful word to be found, and a similar kind of radical compression appears to be at work in the omissions of the final line, making the poem feel like a bathysphere that has ventured too deep into the ocean for its hull to withstand the steadily building pressure. From Auden Murray derives terms and means for communicating in shorthand or code a sense of the panoramic sweep of evolution, which is surely the force exerting the pressure, and she also borrows his cinematic technique of cutting from human distress to the indifference of the universe: 'startled cries', 'barren sands'; 'various city pain', 'receding sky' and 'stars' in orbit. Auden's vision of the innate treachery of civilization is activated by her use of the word 'lie', rhyming with its cosmic antithesis 'sky', in the poem's penultimate line, and as in early Auden, authority of delivery is fused with the opacity of the message: why three cities, three veins, three cries? How can slender clotted veins also be 'inlocked [another nonce word] hands'? Are these hands meant to suggest that the three cities represent intertwined civilizations rising from the barren sands in some system-based reading, like that propounded by Yeats in *A Vision*, of human history? How odd to describe 'barren sands' as having 'sprang'! Might it, one begins to wonder, be as pointless to try to interpret such a poem as it is one by, say, Ern Malley, the fictitious Australian poet created by James McAuley and

Harold Stewart in 1944 as a means of satirizing the obscurity of modern verse?

By 1946 of course, when he decided to award Murray's manuscript the prize, Auden had moved decisively away from the idiom that his pupil sets about reanimating in a poem such as 'If Here in the City'; and Auden would in later life often cast a pretty cold eye on the more vatic aspects of his early work, regretting in particular the influence of Rilke, whom he felt had lured him into writing 'too much Poetry with a capital P'. Yet it was precisely this Poetry with a capital P that Murray, and then, to cite the most obvious example, John Ashbery after her, found at once as invigorating as catnip, and, despite its originator's qualms, an eminently viable way for poetry to happen. It is surely a testimony to Auden's eye for talent, whatever form that talent took, that he selected for the Yale series first Murray's *Poems* and then Ashbery's *Some Trees*, for both make extensive use of a poetic mode that, although he had himself invented it, he had since come to mistrust.

'If Here in the City' is, I think, at once too derivative and too baffling to be classed as one of Murray's stronger efforts, but by placing it at the head of her collection, which contains seventy-six pieces in all, Code allowed her to acknowledge the Audenesque as the portal through which she entered the poetic realms that follow. Most of the volume it inaugurates consists of shortish lyrics, of which about some twenty turn the page. Book Three and Book Seven conclude with Murray's two longest and, in my opinion, two finest works: 'An Epithalamium', which occupies five pages, and 'Orpheus. Three Eclogues', which runs to nine.

While the bleak urgency of the book's opening salvo subliminally reflects the era in which Murray's oeuvre was composed, one finds in her work few specific historical references. An exception to this rule is 'The Coming of Strange People', which is subtitled 'Written on the day of Holland's invasion', allowing us to date it to 10 May, 1940 – some 5 months, that is, before her spell at the New School. But this poem, like 'If Here in the City', is concerned to view the events of history from a dauntingly wide-angled perspective. Certainly it laments the casualties of the invasion ('So many bodies flat upon the stir of spring', it begins) and the return of 'old war chanting', and condemns the 'hate' fuelling the invaders, who, curiously, are never named but simply called 'strange people', as if the speaker were an anthropologist scrupulously adopting the terminology for outsiders of a tribe under scrutiny; but the poem also moves spectacularly beyond the 'bewildered age' she inhabits, contrasting the chaos of the present with nature's powers of recuperation:

> From this land we see the valleys and the banners.
> The hollow places will hold ruins for a time;
> Then the sides of the mountains will green and flower,
> Even women shall bear trees and know the leaves for children.

One is reminded of the attempts of Wallace Stevens to create adequate space for the soldier in his conjugations of the relationship between reality and imagination in his poetry of the war years, in particular of the mixture of human carnage and the irrepressible, exotic energies of nature intertwined in the jungle of 'Asides on the Oboe' of 1940, with its 'jasmine haunted forests' in which the poet hears the central man 'chanting for those buried in their blood'. My guess is that Murray closely read Stevens – about the value of whose work, incidentally, Auden was deeply sceptical; and, if I'm right in this, more incidentally still, by fusing these two antithetical influences she again anticipates the processes that shaped the development of Ashbery.

While Stevens tends to reach, in his meditations on the issues raised by war, towards a delicate balance between the ideal and the real, with self-conscious pointers to the paradigmatic role that poetry can play in negotiations between them, Murray's 'The Coming of Strange People' concludes with a resonant delineation of evolutionary harshness and the crisis of the moment:

> Earth, there is no gentle shaping of the clay.
> Time, no building in the hour.
> Things come and the sea is sea without us.
> All is brash and still, with bone to fallow on,
> And bitter of mouth are we who taste the green this spring.

The gentle pathos of Wilfred Owen's 'Was it for this the clay grew tall?' is firmly set aside by the unsparing rigour of the historical consciousness these lines purvey. Things come, they don't even fall apart, and whatever epithet we apply to the sea, from Homer's 'wine-dark' to Stevens's 'tragic-gestured', affects the sea itself not at all. The only concession to sentiment lies in acknowledging the bitterness of the taste of the spring in May of 1940, with the bones of the dead dispersed like nutrient, lying fallow in its lap.

'The Coming of Strange People' is the opening poem of Book Six, and a number of other pieces in this section explore, or reflect upon, the will to conquest. In 'Ahab the Supermonomaniac' Murray succinctly sums up the corrosive emotions driving Melville's obsessed hero: 'Sought all life damned. / Pain chanted imaginings'. The three poems that follow are all set in England, which is presented by Murray

as already in the throes of post-imperial diminishment, as an
'island-once-kingdom'. 'We were Empire and now we are dead
or Mayflower' she observes in the longest of these, a line which
might be said to compact into ten words Auden's compendious
diagnoses of his mother country, which culminated in his
decision to follow in the footsteps of the pilgrim fathers to
America, rather than collapse, as he feared he otherwise would,
to what he calls in 'Consider' 'a classic fatigue'. It can plausibly
be argued that Auden is Britain's first post-imperial poet, and
something of the historical guilt and fear of lassitude or failure
that drives so much of his thirties poetry infiltrates Murray's
depictions of England too: 'Then know what it is to have the
sins of the father!' she exclaims in 'Empire Now Dead and
Mayflower' – Code presumably quarried the poem's title from
the line quoted above. 'On Looking at Left Fields' ('left' here
meaning 'abandoned') enjoins us to note how in 'the old fields
the old corn tangles', and the 'sleek weed twists and strangles',
ruining 'lands' that once were 'green'. In this poem, another
set of three quatrains rhyming ABAB, Murray shifts from a
sense of national inertia and inadequacy to an image of herself
as a Londoner, one who knows from the inside, the symptoms
of the national malaise:

> Dried leaves like lizard scales over the land
> And the slow blink down to winter.
> Father of shivering times, crazed by each spring's demand,
> Why would you know your daughter?
>
> It is this London they will never know –
> Something of must, stale bread and spring,
> The fattened dog, the thinning child and Rotten Row.
> To be born a Londoner, as I, gives meaning to the thing.

Are the 'they', one can't help wondering, her transatlantic relations? This poem is followed by 'London', a wonderful piece of urban description that I much regret not including in my anthology *London: A History in Verse*. 'London sits with her hands cupped', it begins. What is the personified city waiting for? Pigeons, sparrows, a 'fat-flanked mare', 'slim weeds of ivy' animate its streets and buildings, along with Easter lilies, only for all to be suddenly obliterated by the capricious spring weather:

> a cool breeze speaks out of some darker street,
> Clouds shuffle up with restless intrepidity, and spill
> Their whole river of abundance at her feet,
> The whole clean wide river, and wrap her in one river of sleet,
> Her sides in one wet sheet.

As such lines demonstrate, Murray's poetry is adept, perhaps too relentlessly for some, at making the strange familiar and the familiar strange. Rhyme often plays a distinctive role in her creation of oblique angles and surprising twists, as in the chiming here of *street / feet / sleet / sheet*. She frequently makes superb use of off-rhyme too, as well as of variable line lengths, whose effect in her work is memorably described by Ashbery as 'suggestive of waves washing up on a beach, with every so often an unusually long one, like the wave that surprises you when you're walking by the ocean, making you run to escape it'.

For all their whimsy and wanderings, Murray's poems come in carefully structured shapes and sizes; her curious swoops and zigzags develop within elastic but recognizable stanza patterns, often allowing an energizing tension between impulse and rigour to emerge. 'What will the wish, what will the dance do?' inquires Auden at the end of his short poem 'Orpheus' of 1937, and while not exactly a formalist, Murray shows herself insistently aware of how the dance can liberate the wish. Indeed a number of her poems proffer as an image of the maker not an inspired bard but a toiling architect. The second half of Book One consists of six poems in a row that develop architectural themes as a means of foregrounding the relationship between the fluidity of the imagination and the structures that seem in opposition to its freedoms. 'It is the action of water that is the nearest thing to man', exclaim the young in the opening lines of 'The Builder', to which a 'sullen cry', which I take to be that of the builder himself, responds that there is 'no time to stop in the work and the job, only time to breathe, / And breathe in your own fine sweat'. A fairly standard antithesis seems set up here, but the poem goes on to complicate it in a range of intriguing ways. Appealing as the indolent young's resistance to work and order may seem, how far, the poem asks, can one take the romantic ideal of the imagination as formless and insatiable? 'I want to wander over the hills', enthuses its Orphic speaker,

> and down to the water,
> And if there is sea I want to pack it up in my arms,
> And let the blue globe of all the wide water fill my mouth
> Till my jaw hangs loose, and come piling into me,
> Fill up my head, my chest, and the sea-filled loins to burst in me.

The builder may be sullen, and his constructions doomed, but as the poem's last stanza makes clear, he is more aware than the absurdly water-inflated speaker of what he is doing. 'We're building', he explains,

towers of Babel that will crumble down before dawn,
Like the falling of water down and down to the sea,
And we'd die making towers of Babel while they tumble down
to the sea.'

This may not achieve quite the defiant splendour of Yeats's 'All things fall and are built again, / And those that build them again are gay'; nevertheless, the extravagant, almost parodic terms in which Murray stages this dialogue between romantic impulse and classical form indicate a high degree of self-consciousness about her own procedures, and suggest the need to move beyond the high rhetoric of modernism towards more indeterminate and flexible styles of approach to the relationship between desire and convention.

Murray's conjugations of the figure of the architect in these poems connect with the overall vision that the book presents of the history of civilization and its culmination in the modern city. In the first in the series the Gothic is celebrated for its power to incorporate into its facades architecture's seeming opposite, the 'passions of night', in the gargoyle shape of a chuckling 'slippery imp' or 'a fangy slit-eyed creature of no race'. A 'little architect' is rocked to sleep in another that Murray – or Code – called 'Lullaby', which is about a mother and child rather than the fickle lovers presented in Auden's poem of the same name. As in the last stanza of Auden's love poem, Murray's 'Lullaby' delicately dreams a happy future for its addressee, imagining the future structures that she will one day build fusing as successfully as Gothic cathedrals the organic and irrational with the 'dead' stone of which they are made:

The grass will not be so insignificant, the stone so dead.
You will spiral up the mansions we have sown.
Drop your lids, little architect. Admit the bats of wisdom into
    your head.

The looping parabolas made by bats offer a useful way of figuring Murray's poetic imagination as a whole. No doubt the kinds of wisdom it conveys may seem to some a little skittish or elusive – although she is by no means averse to accumulating series of propositions that appear to be aiming at the lapidary or epigrammatic. The short poem 'Men and Women Have Meaning Only as Man and Woman' consists entirely of such propositions, but ones that manage to combine the self-evident and the unfathomable, or at the very least, unverifiable, like a miscellany of mistranslated koans or a set of philosophical exempla that one can't quite follow:

Men and women have meaning only as man and woman.
The moon is itself and it is lost among stars.
The days are individual, and in the passage
The nights are each sleep, but the dreams vary.
A repeated action is upon its own feet.
We who have spoken there speak here.

It is not easy to take issue with such statements; their wisdom lies in the sense they communicate of a kind of false bottom to our uses of language. Like Auden, Murray is not afraid of giving full reign to the urge to define and categorize, yet the seemingly systematic processes of assertion and illustration that inform her poems tend to register as subtly but irretrievably askew, as 'makeshift', to adopt Code's term, despite the authoritative tones in which they are delivered. 'Men and

Women ...' concludes:

> The timing of independent objects
> Permits them to live and move and admit their space
> And entity and various attitudes of life.
> All things are cool in themselves and complete.

If the 'cool' tone reminds one of Wittgenstein's dispassionate chains of logic in the *Tractatus*, the lacunae that open up between each of the poem's sentences suggest a mind pursuing certainties where none exist.

It is lack of completion, however, that drives her two longest pieces, 'An Epithalamium' and 'Orpheus. Three Eclogues', which both explore relationships between men and women, or man and woman. 'An Epithalamium' is subtitled 'Or Marriage Day in a Little-Known Country / A Marriage Poem for an Age', and is in the form of a dialogue between The Young Women and The Young Men of this little-known country. The ceremonial aspect of the epithalamium tradition is honoured, up to a point, in the poem's formal properties: the first four alternating speeches are 13 lines long, as is the sixth, which is spoken by The Young Men; the fifth, and the concluding seventh, both spoken by The Young Women, are seventeen lines long. Perhaps, in this little-known country, this is the form taken by all epithalamiums.

The poem attempts, rather like Auden's very early charade *Paid on Both Sides*, which developed out of his reading of Icelandic sagas, to use the archaic and immemorial to delineate a radically modern sensibility. Both are anatomies of late adolescence, of its fantasies and uncertainties and trembling fascination with new kinds of linguistic and empirical possibility, but while Auden's charade harks back to the japes of a public school Junior Common Room or the rituals of Officer Training Corps, Murray's young women and young men float free of any particular social context. In numerous passages the influence of Rilke, especially of the *Duino Elegies*, is strong, but not, I think, overpowering:

> On the hill we see a child plucking flowers:
> The round face of the day is seeded with infinities.
> In our minds the children stamp, the strict parent frowns, the
>   infant cowers
> Behind random clusters, the flower-symbol, to smother
>   laughter.
> Compact and kneeling, we smoothe the wet grass to one side,
> Learning to touch the earth with consideration,
> Knowing that we must be less militant and young to stroke the
>   things that hide.
> Even the bright dew weeps from the stem at our inept and
>   thoughtless touch.

The novelty and the clumsiness of awakening sexual consciousness are beautifully captured in such lines. The pastoral tradition, which dominates Book Three in Code's arrangement, is elegantly and boldly reconfigured throughout these seven monologues, which interact with each other in an oblique but effective way, rather in the manner of the speeches by the four characters of Auden's *The Age of Anxiety* (a poem subtitled a 'A Baroque Eclogue') on which he was at work during the summer that he selected Murray's poems for the Yale prize. 'An Epithalamium' is Murray's fullest exploration of what I called in relation to 'Believe Me, My Fears Are Ancient' the procreative urge. At many moments the writing turns frankly erotic: 'Come, O come to us', urge The Young

Women in the final section, 'so that we shall know more of the pine against the hill'. Whatever her health problems, Murray was as capable as, say, the Keats of 'The Eve of St Agnes' of imagining the coming together of lovers and their mutual transformation by this act of blending into new identities that move beyond the scope or reach of the poem: 'And they are gone – ay, ages long ago / These lovers fled away into the storm', observes Keats in his final stanza; 'Lovers may touch,' 'An Epithalamium' concludes, 'but the marriage bond is a link without distraction'.

Except, of course, when one of the lovers dies. In 'Orpheus. Three Eclogues', the volume's last poem, Murray bravely picks up the myth that Rilke had made spectacularly his own, first in 'Orpheus. Eurydice. Hermes' and then in *The Sonnets to Orpheus*. Murray's poem has a wider cast list, including Orpheus's mother Calliope, Charon, who punts him across the Acheron, as well as the Beasts that Orpheus enchants and the Shades of Hades, who are both given a choric role. If 'An Epithalamium' recreates the vivid pulse of dawning sexuality that animates Keats's 'The Eve of St Agnes', Murray's Eurydice comes to resemble the mournful knight of 'La Belle Dame Sans Merci', hollowed out by the failure of love, stranded, by Orpheus's sudden change of mind, in the world of the Shades. As they proceed on the path up from Hades, Eurydice gradually recovers her sensuality and humanity, imagining, like a convalescent taking her first tottering steps out of bed, the life she is about to recover:

> I will lean myself to the wind and nibble the sensation,
> Passionately grasp the oval bowls of wine,
> Taste and tamper, have precise delight in the minutest tilt of
> inclination.

Much of the poem, with the exception of the choric passages, makes cleverly unobtrusive use of Murray's favoured ABAB rhyme scheme, although this breaks down in the two lines that Eurydice utters as Orpheus turns, the most affecting lines, to my mind, in her entire oeuvre:

> In my palms lie these two clear efforts of my eyes,
> The very essence of this tormented moment.

As 'An Epithalamium' found a complex but ceremonial language in which to translate The Young Women and The Young Men's approach to sexual union, so this decisive moment of sundering is conveyed in a calm, uplifting, almost metaphysical image. Orpheus's decision to turn to look at his wife and thus condemn her to return to Pluto is made no more explicable by Murray than the sudden onset of a deadly illness, while the choric summation by The Shades, which brings the poem, and the volume as a whole, to a close, returns us to the remorseless cosmic perspectives of the opening piece, 'If Here in the City':

> Birds and beasts, rocks and fish of the sea,
> Watch how the lidless pools absorb to themselves
> The improbable adventure without a ripple.

Death quietly claims Eurydice, however frantically Orpheus clutches her vanishing image, and then afterwards laments her loss. The poem is clear that never again will the border between death and life prove porous: 'Leave what may be the absolute of death to us, the proper dead'.

Murray's book seems to me a startling achievement for a poet who died at an even younger age than Keats, a month short of her twenty-fifth birthday. It is surprising, particularly after John Ashbery's eloquent praise of her work in 2003, that she has attracted so little critical attention, by which I actually mean none: this essay is, as far as I can tell, the first ever written on her oeuvre. The improbable poetic adventures her *Poems* offers have slipped into oblivion, like Eurydice, almost without a ripple, although she does make cameo appearances in David Lehman's *The Oxford Book of American Poetry* of 2006 and Evan Jones and Todd Swift's *Modern Canadian Poets* of 2010. Auden ends his short Foreword by recommending four pieces to a casual browser of *Poems* in a bookstore: these are 'You Talk of Art', 'An Epithalamium', 'Even the Gulls of the Cool Atlantic', and 'Orpheus'. 'I am confident', he adds, 'that, if he is a true judge and lover of poetry, he will neither leave the store without taking the volume with him, nor ever regret his purchase'. It can take a while to tune in to the 'fluctuant', to borrow one of her favourite adjectives, manoeuvres that Murray's poems perform, but Auden is surely right to suggest that those who make the effort will not regret it. 'Admit', as the mother advises her little architect in 'Lullaby', 'the bats of wisdom into your head'.

Poetry (2014)

Acknowledgements

Acknowledgements are due to the various publications in which these essays and reviews originally appeared, sometimes in slightly different forms and with different titles:

London Review of Books: 'Walt Whitman's Democratic Vistas'; 'The Double Vision of Baudelaire'; 'Ezra Pound's Letters Home'; 'A.S.J. Tessimond and Bernard Spencer'; 'Child Randall'.

New York Review of Books: 'Fevers of the Bone: John Donne'; 'Owls, Bicycles, Bailiffs: The Pataphysical Life of Alfred Jarry'; 'Dark Caverns: The Correspondence of T.S. Eliot'; 'Industrious Auden' (all reprinted with permission from *The New York Review of Books*. Copyright © 2009-2011-2012–13).

New Walk: 'Who Seekest Thy Woob? Samuel Greenberg and Hart Crane'.

Poetry: 'Joan Murray and the Bats of Wisdom'.

The Oxford Handbook of Victorian Poetry, edited by Matthew Bevis (OUP, 2013): 'City of Pain: The Poetry of James Thomson'.

Mark Ford has published four volumes of poetry, *Landlocked* (1992), *Soft Sift* (2001), *Six Children* (2011) and *Selected Poems* (2014). He has also written a biography of the French poet, playwright and novelist Raymond Roussel, and translated Roussel's *New Impressions of Africa*. His anthology, *London: A History in Verse*, was published in 2012. He is a regular contributor to the *London Review of Books* and the *New York Review of Books*. *This Dialogue of One* is his third collection of essays. He teaches in the English Department at University College London.

EYEWEAR PUBLISHING